Rockingham Park

1933–1969

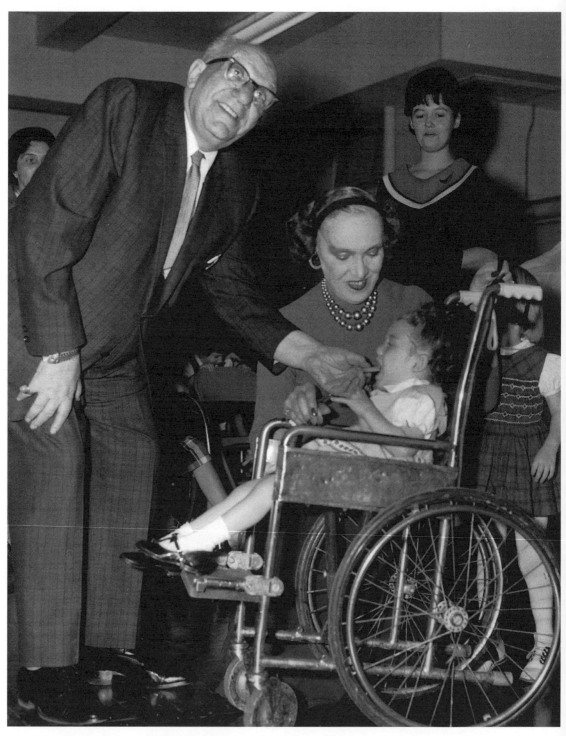

Lou and Lutza Smith gave generously of their time and money to improve the lives of disabled children.

Rockingham Park
1933–1969

A History of Power, Glamour, and Gambling

Paul Peter Jesep

Published for
THE LOU AND LUTZA SMITH FOUNDATION

by
Peter E. Randall Publisher
Portsmouth, New Hampshire
1998

Peter E. Randall Publisher
Box 4726
Portsmouth, NH 03802-4726
Design: Tom Allen

Front endleaves: Rockingham Park in late 1930s.
Rear endleaves: The old paddock at Rockingham Park.

Library of Congress Cataloging-in-Publication Data

Jesep, Paul Peter.
Rockingham Park, 1933-1969 : a history of power, glamour, and gambling / Paul Peter Jesep.
    p. cm.
Includes bibliographical references (p.) and index.
ISBN 0-914339-71-0 (alk. paper)
    1. Rockingham Park (Salem, N.H.)—History. I. Title.
SF324.35.N4J47   1998
798.4'006'87426—dc21

                                                          98-38803
                                                          CIP

Foreword

As the Lou and Lutza Smith Charitable Foundation concluded its work within the fifteen year span specified by the Smiths for its duration, the Trustees of the Foundation explored various options toward providing a suitable memorial to the Smiths and their impact on New Hampshire. Among the ideas considered, but discarded, were commissioning a history of the Smiths themselves and writing a history of the Charitable Foundation that they established after their deaths.

The option chosen by the Trustees, the work that you are about to read, was to commission a history of Rockingham Park, focusing on its economic impact upon the State of New Hampshire during the Smith's ownership of the track. Since it was upon Rockingham Park that the Smiths built their wealth, the Trustees determined that it would be an appropriate testimonial to the couple to commission a history of the Park, particularly since such a thorough history had never been undertaken.

The Trustees chose for this task a young professional, Paul Peter Jesep, who is an attorney, a journalist, and a writer. The Trustees did not impose any restrictions on Mr. Jesep, but rather asked him to devote his attention to the task in any manner that he thought appropriate. In addition to the records of the Lou and Lutza Smith Charitable Foundation, Mr. Jesep had available to him many of the records of the Park still extant at the track facility in Salem, New Hampshire.

Mr. Jesep conducted many interviews with individuals involved with the track, including some of New Hampshire's leading politicians. I think you will find that the result of Mr. Jesep's efforts supplies the reader with much information about the impact of the track on New Hampshire's economic life. It also makes for a very entertaining read.

I hope you enjoy this book as much as I did.

CHARLES A. DEGRANDPRE, CHAIR
Lou and Lutza Smith Charitable Foundation
April 1998

Contents

Acknowledgments

Atty. Charles A. DeGrandpre, of McLane, Graf, Raulerson & Middleton and chair of the Lou and Lutza Smith Foundation, was the driving force behind this project. He recognized the significant impact Rockingham Park had on New Hampshire's politics and economy. From the very beginning, he envisioned a book to record, celebrate, and document the track's important contributions to the Granite State. I'm honored to have been part of this project. And I'm especially grateful for Atty. DeGrandpre's friendship.

Former governors Hugh Gregg and Walter Peterson; former state attorney general Jeffrey R. Howard; Richard Broussard, editor in chief for Network Publications and *New Hampshire Editions*; Dean Dexter, contributing editor for Network Publications and *New Hampshire Editions*; and especially Michael P. Chaney, chief operating officer for the New Hampshire Historical Society, made many important editorial suggestions.

Many individuals shared colorful stories about Lou and Lutza Smith, and these interviews provided much insight. These people include Charles DeGrandpre; Louise Newman; Governors Hugh Gregg, Walter Peterson, and Lane Dwinell; Stewart Lamprey; Mike Dagostino; Ernie Barka; Alan Pope; Douglas Seed; and Atty. Robert A. Shaines.

Edward Callahan, vice president and general manager of Rockingham Park, deserves a particular debt of gratitude. He not only reviewed the manuscript, but more importantly also permitted me to comb through the files and photos of Rockingham Park. Much of the documentation contained in this book stems from the track's archives. Lynne Snierson, also of Rockingham Park, provided valuable assistance in preparing this book as well. The walking tour she gave me was especially appreciated.

Frank Wright, curator of manuscripts for the Nevada State Museum and Historical Society, provided invaluable information about Lou Smith's Las Vegas track. He also provided a script used by a local Public Radio station on Lou Smith's Nevada track.

Mary Kuechenmeister penned a fine Epilogue to this book. Jo R. Catalino, secretary to Attorney DeGrandpre, has helped to shepherd this project along.

Tim Mason, administrative secretary for the Commissioners/Budget Office of the State of New Hampshire, provided the General Fund Budget Appropriations figures used extensively in this book.

Peter E. Randall is a splendid publisher and Doris Troy an exceptional editor. Both made important contributions.

Finally, Atty. Harry Nelson Starbranch Jr., a law school classmate, and his family, first shared with me some of the beauty and rich heritage of New Hampshire.

In Memory of Maria Jesep—"Moya Baba"

Lou Smith–patriarch of New England Thoroughbred racing.

CHAPTER I

Power, Money, and Glitz

Noting the tremendous revenue the State of New Hampshire was deriving from racing, Rhode Island and Massachusetts moved in . . . Racing is now legalized in 26 states and each year the combined revenue to these states is in excess of $125 million . . . money that otherwise would have to come from tax-payers' pockets.

B.A. Dario, President of Lincoln Downs, 1952[1]

Lou Smith, the gruff but compassionate founder and driving force behind Salem's Rockingham Park, is widely recognized for bringing world class thoroughbred racing and legalized pari-mutuel gambling to New England. Even more importantly, but often overlooked, Smith's track, over a thirty-five year period, employed, directly or indirectly, thousands of people (including more than fifty members of the state legislature at one time or another), generated the revenue that helped to keep New Hampshire government afloat (see Table A), and pumped millions of dollars into the economy by purchasing locally made products to satisfy its thousands of patrons. Between 1933 and 1969, Rockingham Park generated an average annual amount comprising 20 percent of the state's General Fund Budget Appropriations.

Rockingham Park also became the social capital of New Hampshire, attracting political leaders, sports legends, Hollywood celebrities and entertainers, some of the nation's top thoroughbred breeders, and even the Roman Catholic Cardinal of Boston, Richard J. Cushing. The cardinal regularly visited the track and developed a close friendship with its Jewish general manager. "There's no question about it," reflected former House Speaker and Senate President Stewart Lamprey: "It was one of the grand places of New Hampshire."[2]

Lou and Lutza Smith, enigmatic and introverted in many ways, maintained a high public profile when it came to philanthropy. Unable to have children of their own, they worked tirelessly to help disabled youngsters. They also

During WWI the closed track was used to house and train soldiers before they were shipped overseas.

assisted many of New Hampshire's religious communities, among many other charities, during economic downturns. Despite their very public roles, though, some mystery still surrounds Lou and Lutza, who seemed to be somewhat guarded about their past.

"The Rock's" dramatic impact on the cultural, economic, and political fabric of the Granite State has never been fully told. An ongoing conservative

Waiting to fight Kaiser Wilhelm's troops.

view of gambling, still prevalent today, may have minimized its significant contributions to the state. Hence, historians looked to other aspects of New Hampshire's rich heritage to record and embrace. Many upstanding families, normally opposed to gambling, built businesses, and in some cases fortunes because of Rockingham Park. The Rock's patrons needed services, and Lou Smith decided to trade with certain fledgling businesses.

Salem, once a sleepy town, became a thriving city due, in part, to the wealth generated by what many considered a vice.[3] In the end, Rockingham Park left an indelible, positive impression on the New Hampshire landscape. "When you talk about Rockingham Park," said Alan Pope, chief of staff to Governors Lane Dwinell and Hugh Gregg, "you touch the soul of New Hampshire in what I'd call the good old days."[4]

Rockingham County Commissioner and former vice chair of the House Ways and Means Committee Ernie Barka reflected, "Rockingham Park is a

The Rock as it looked when owned by John W. Gates and John A. Drake in 1906.

very important part of New Hampshire history. From 1933 to 1969 Lou Smith and Rockingham was the story. Lou Smith and the track. There wasn't anything more important in New Hampshire."[5]

The track fostered an ongoing debate of how it could assist state government to grapple with a plethora of problems that still dominate sessions of the General Court. New Hampshire, for now, remains opposed to a broadbased sales or income tax. But to maintain this position, many state public-policy analysts insist that government faces increasing challenges to generating revenue.

Today, gambling is still viewed as a possible solution to the state's fiscal challenges: witness the debate over video gambling in the 1996 gubernatorial election. In 1997, the State Supreme Court's decision that funding education with property taxes is unconstitutional has made policymakers reexamine revenue-raising mechanisms. This includes reevaluating New Hampshire's long held anti-broadbased tax position.

Debating the merits of a broadbased tax date to 1927. In that year Gov. Huntley N. Spaulding appointed a group of lawmakers to the Recess Tax Commission to make recommendations regarding the financing of government. In a ten year period (1918-1928) the expenditures of state and local government had more than doubled. The costs of education and highways alone rose from $11.5 million to $23.5 million. Land served as the primary tax source to finance government. To a lesser degree, corporate, lumber, and electric utility franchise taxes, along with motor vehicle permits, also generated revenue.[6]

A year after its appointment, the commission concluded that the "total amount of state, county and local taxes in this state is at the present time in excess of $20,000,000 per annum . . . This is all New Hampshire can afford, and we should regard any increase in it as extravagance." The commission however, recommended that a broadbased income tax be adopted to equalize the tax burden.[7] The recommendation never became law. And shortly after reaching this decision, New Hampshire's fiscal plight worsened with the start of the Great Depression.

Although it could hardly be imagined at the time, an abandoned horse track in a quiet community would save the state from fiscal collapse and dramatically change New Hampshire's social, political, and economic environment.

In 1931, Lou Smith and a few partners purchased Rockingham Park. Originally opened as a horse track in 1906, the first owners, John W. Gates and John A. Drake, were forced to close it not long thereafter. The state refused to allow Gates and Drake to hold pari-mutuel gambling races.[8]

Similarly, Smith and his colleagues were closed down, shortly after their 1931 purchase, because they incorrectly assumed that the state's position on the issue had changed. But rather than sell the track, Smith sensed an opportunity as the state and national economies continued to worsen.[9] His instincts about making a buck would prove correct.

In 1933, two years after his decision to keep the track (which remained closed during this period), New Hampshire's unemployment rate hovered at 33 percent. In 1930, the state had an overall population of 465,293.[10] Not surprisingly, the drop in wages caused tax revenue to plummet. Exacerbating the problem were the 40,000 *additional* men, women, and children receiving some form of social assistance from the state[11] since the stock market's crash in 1929.

Lou Smith judiciously used his time during the Rock's two-year dormancy to form alliances and friendships in Concord. This networking, coupled with the pressures of an economic depression, made the political and legislative environment perfect for a pari-mutuel gambling bill. In 1933, a bill legalizing gambling at the Salem track passed both houses of the General Court.

On Monday, April 3, 1933, Gov. John G. Winant, desperate to generate tax revenue, reluctantly allowed the bill to become law without his signature.[12] The state would receive a percentage of the betting handle.[13] Lou Smith had not just succeeded in getting gambling legalized; he also obtained a monopoly on it that would last almost four decades.

Winant was likely and justifiably very concerned that organized crime would get a solid foothold in New Hampshire. Such notorious thugs as Waxey Gordon, Dutch Shultz, Lucky Luciano, and Ralph "The Pimp" Liguori were making headlines throughout the nation for extortion, prostitution rings, underground beer halls, and, of course, gambling operations. The Great Depression created an environment ripe for such social ills, which contributed to the corruption of political figures, police departments, and the populace in general.[14]

In addition to the uneasiness this possible scenario caused, the governor must have looked on the recent past with much angst. In 1931, he created a road program that put three thousand men to work. In the same year, he must have lamented as weekly payrolls in Berlin dropped from $235,000 to $50,000. "Toward the end of the winter," wrote historian Bernard Bellush, "with freezing cold and snow still blanketing the North Country, Chairman James Langley of the Governor's Committee on Unemployment conceded for the first time that malnutrition was a reality in many Granite State homes. With every third worker in the state unemployed, Winant moved sharply in the direction of experimental responses to the Great Depression."[15]

Over the weekend of April 1, 1933, Winant, as he wrestled with the pros and cons of the gambling bill, confronted further grim news. Nothing in the newspapers indicated that the national depression would end soon or that New Hampshire's high unemployment rate would drop in the near future.

That spring, the City of Manchester negotiated a 6 percent loan from the Amoskeag Manufacturing Company due to the "banking holiday" called by President Franklin D. Roosevelt. In Concord, two hundred stonecutters went on strike to protest the reduction of wages from $8 to $6.80 a day. President Roosevelt indicated that he would sign a bill cutting $400 million in annual benefits to war veterans. And Sheriff George A. Wooster, of Merrimack County, refused to reappoint twelve deputies because it would not "be fair to appoint men as deputies, if appropriations are not sufficient to enable them to earn their livings."[16]

In this deteriorating environment, Winant had passively consented to give Lou Smith's racetrack an exclusive gambling license. One Granite Stater in Concord lamented after the bill became law: "When they passed a law lettin' folks play baste ball o' Sundays, two year ago, I thought mebbe we was gettin' close to the Jedgment Day. And now they're a-goin' to let 'em bet on hoss races right here in New Hampsheer! No, sir it don't seem possible!"[17]

At a town meeting in Salem about two weeks after Winant allowed the bill to become law, residents voted in favor of gambling by a margin of 617 to 2.[18] The law provided that the General Court would renew the gambling license every two years. But as the Rock's importance as a job and revenue source for the state increased, the legislature renewed the license for far longer periods of time. Eventually, renewal became nothing more than a formality.

On April 3, 1933, with the passage of legalized gambling, began one of the most colorful and controversial periods of New Hampshire's history. While the state clearly needed the tax revenue generated by Rockingham Park, there was a trade-off. Granite Staters had to accept the enormous power that one man, Lou Smith, had in politics and on legislative issues, even though he used his clout with discretion. The track owner also masterfully manipulated and directed public opinion through his legendary philanthropy. And the public knew it. In addition, many Granite Staters grappled with another ethical dilemma for much of the track's existence: to accept gambling and perhaps compromise individual or community standards of morality, or oppose gambling and lose badly needed revenue. In the end, as it often does, the almighty dollar decided the issue.

CHAPTER 2

Economic Impact of the Rock

Former House Speaker and Senate President Stewart Lamprey quipped, "We ran the state on booze, butts, and bets."[19] Rockingham Park, during Lou Smith's tenure as general manager (1933-1969), generated more than $108 million in tax revenue for the state. This figure comprises $86,948,558 from thoroughbred racing and another $21,766,672 from harness racing. Tax revenue from the latter source didn't begin until 1958.[20]

In 1934, a year after the Rock began filling state coffers, almost 21 percent of the General Fund Budget Appropriations came from pari-mutuel thoroughbred gambling. During the last year of World War II, 46.75 percent of the General Fund Budget Appropriations came from tax revenue generated at the Rock! In 1969, the year of Lou Smith's death, almost 13 percent of the General Fund Budget Appropriations came from the Salem track.[21]

SALEM

Although passage of the pari-mutuel bill didn't generate instantaneous wealth for the state treasury, it did have an immediate impact on Salem. William Barron, chairman of the Salem Board of Selectman and later one of Smith's employees, told the press that he expected to see one of the largest economic windfalls for the region in years.[22] The *Manchester Leader* reported that "a number of real estate transactions, which have been dependent upon the opening of the track, are about to be consummated."[23] A few hours after learning of Governor Winant's decision not to veto the bill, Lou Smith ordered several hundred trees to beautify the track and made a large order for lumber. Within months, the Rock had new stables, renovated buildings, and a resurfaced track.[24]

The renovation, the first of several over the next thirty-five years, cost $400,000 by opening day. More than 500 men were employed for the task. They received $200,000 in wages. Among the items built were roads to the track ($50,000), a jockey house ($5,000), and a clubhouse ($25,000).[25] When these improvements were completed, almost 1,700 Granite Staters applied for 220 jobs at Rockingham Park.[26]

By 1940, Salem's tax rate was the lowest it had been in seven years. According to an article in the *Peterborough Transcript*, "Relief rolls have been cut to the bone . . . More money has been spent on schools and roads, and a town deficit has been turned into a town surplus." The track paid almost a half million dollars in operating salaries and also added to the local economy "in the ordinary channels of every-day business," the article continued. The Rock purchased everything from fertilizer to soap to office supplies from local merchants.[27]

"Any kid in Salem could have a job at Rockingham Park," observed Mike Dagostino, a Republican activist and a state employee charged with making sure that a large number of track employees were Granite Staters. Or if slots were filled, someone would call Sam Simon, operator of the concession stand at the Rock for many years (as well as the one at the Boston Garden), to place a hard-working Salem youngster.[28]

The Rock's economic clout automatically created political influence, permitting it to direct all publicpolicy initiatives relating to gambling. The state highway department, for example, directed that Route 111 be laid out from Exeter to Nashua.

The new road gave the Maine/New Hampshire seacoast access to Salem. "This new route," observed a reporter, "will furnish the most practical way to get to the Rockingham racetrack from this vicinity [the seacoast] in the future."[29]

About twenty years later, Interstate 93 linked Salem with the rest of the world. Gov. Wesley Powell appointed a special committee to decide whether a special "spur" should connect Rockingham Park with the highway. Salem's selectmen and planning board were involved in the decision making process.[30] Frederick W. Rovenkamp, of the *Rochester Courier*, wrote, "The presence of the million dollar Rockingham Park horse racetrack is manifest in town government, in the community's economic life, and in the attitude of the citizens. The entire Salem Board of Selectmen is on the payroll of the gambling plant."[31] Not surprisingly, the special committee ultimately found in favor of building the connector.

Interstate 93 saved twenty to thirty minutes in driving time for Rock patrons from the Boston area.[32] The new highway connector led to a substantial rise in business. And as a result, Lou Smith expanded the Rock's parking lot to accommodate 1,500 more cars.[33]

In 1961, 12 percent of Salem's municipal budget came directly from taxes and license fees generated at the track. The Rock's payroll for Salem residents alone exceeded $418,000.[34] In 1967, near the end of Lou Smith's life, the track was Salem's biggest property taxpayer, paying the town $286,846.17. (The Granite State Electric Co. came in a distant second with $63,160.63.[35]) In 1968 and

FACTS
about
ROCKINGHAM PARK
that you as a
New Hampshire
TAXPAYER
should know
1933-1937
435,886
People came
from Boston
by trains to
Rockingham Park

Rockingham Park has brought hundreds of thousands of people and millions of dollars into New Hampshire from other states. In the five years from 1933 to 1937 - Rockingham Park paid the State of New Hampshire

$2,439,487.99 IN TAXES

This money has been applied to a sinking fund for payment of interest charges and reduction of the State's bonded debt. Rockingham Park is one of New Hampshire's assets.

ROCKINGHAM PARK
SALEM, NEW HAMPSHIRE
FALL MEET—SEPTEMBER 12th TO OCTOBER 12th

Fact sheets put concrete figures in the mind's of taxpayers about the Rock's impact on taxes.

1973, the track complained loudly of an unfair property tax rate, but overall, relations between the track and Salem generally remained good.[36]

Horse track gambling had a rippling impact on the entire local economy. Ed Costello, writing for the *Boston Herald* noted that: "A year ago [1958] in an area populated by 6,200,000 people these four tracks (Suffolk Downs, Rockingham Park, Narragansett Park and Lincoln Downs) attracted 2,680,412 fans who wagered $196,539,322. From this amount $14,055,431.70 was trimmed and went into state treasuries . . . When you read about this or that racing track attracting big crowds and handling huge sums of betting money, remember there are many other businesses sharing the windfall."[37]

*Lou Smith, far right, with local and state officials cutting the ceremonial ribbon
to open the Interstate 93 link.*

In 1933, the total racing handle at Rockingham Park exceeded $11 million for
a fifty-four day season. This constituted a daily average of $220,470. In 1946, the
racing handle passed the $56 million mark for a sixty-six day season, the daily
average reached $851,923. In 1970, one year after Lou Smith's death, the total han-
dle reached $67 million for a seventy-seven day thoroughbred season, the daily
average exceeded $870,000.[38] And these figures do not reflect the additional
money patrons spent on gas, motels, restaurants, and other goods and services.

Salem writer and historian Douglas Seed recalls vividly what the Rock
meant to his grandmother's trailer park. "The track brought its own economy
with it. Two-thirds of the people living in the trailer park were track people,"
Seed remembers. "They were there just for the summer." If his grandmother,
Evelyn Birche, had difficulty collecting payment from someone working at the
track, "we could call the racing secretary and the rent would be paid. They
always went out of their way to show that it was a clean operation. One phone
call to the track and the rent was paid,"[39] said Seed. Evelyn Birche's trailer park
closed every year shortly after the track ended its season.

According to County Commissioner Ernie Barka, "[Rockingham Park]
play[ed] an important role in tourism. In those days [it seemed] we had more

Give them a reason and they shall come. The Rock's parking lot brimming to capacity.

motels than we have today. The thing that kept them going was the racetrack. People rented cabins near several lakes around Salem—they came up for two weeks just for the track."[40]

"There are countless fellows out there who went to law school, became doctors, or became teachers because of Rockingham Park," said Mike Dagostino.[41]

Construction projects pumped millions into the local economy and retained the goodwill of all Granite Staters and, just as importantly, maintained the Salem track as the best in New England. Shortly after winning the General Court's approval for the re-renewal of the track's gambling license in 1939, Smith embarked on another face-lift for the track, this one worth $150,000, that included a remodeled grandstand and mezzanine.[42]

The construction of a new clubhouse in 1956 received accolades not just for its structural beauty, but also for its direct and indirect impact on the state. In Salem alone, Peever's Pharmacy, Gelt's Super Market, Leo's Barber Shop, Salem Taxi Service, Blue Bird Bowling Alleys, and the Granite State Potato Chip Co. were among the businesses that publicly paid tribute to Smith for his contributions to the community[43] with a large newspaper ad.

In 1961, Smith began still another modernization project, this time costing

$1.6 million.[44] The additional crowds brought by Interstate 93 made the project imperative. Space for the grandstand increased by 54 percent, the mezzanine by 150 percent, and 520 box seats were added to the clubhouse.[45]

Salem received an economic windfall from Rockingham Park. Not only did the track save the town from the despair caused by the Great Depression, but it also helped to turn the quiet community into an economic engine for south-central New Hampshire. In 1931, Salem had a population of 2,318. Approximately ten years later it had more than 3,200 residents.[46] Between 1950 and 1960, Salem's population increased from 4,805 to 9,210.[47]

NEW HAMPSHIRE

Shortly after the track's opening on June 21, 1933, Lou Smith sent a letter to Gen. Hugh S. Johnson, administrator of the National Recovery Act (NRA), to enroll the track in a program that put able-bodied, unemployed people to work. "We are willing to comply with all regulations," wrote Smith, "and ready to do our part in helping President Roosevelt's wonderful drive on to prosperity and we hope other racetracks throughout the country will follow in our footsteps." Smith concluded, ". . . may . . . prosperity be at the end of the trail."[48] To further assist families hurt by the Depression, he initiated New Hampshire Welfare Day. On this day, all gate receipts, food and program sales, and the track's share of pari-mutuel betting were donated to the state for economically hard-pressed citizens.[49]

This suggests the positive financial impact Rockingham Park had on the state, but even more importantly for Smith, it laid the foundation for a public relations campaign that continued throughout his life, to win and keep the hearts of Granite Staters. In the course of his life, Smith never missed an opportunity to extend assistance to a charity or to an individual. Although sincere in the generosity, it also made his racetrack a good corporate citizen—a reputation needed in a state reluctant to sanction gambling.

In an era when farming was a common career path, some of the tax revenue generated from the Rock went directly to subsidize agricultural fairs. In 1940, nine major state fairs received more than $37,000.[50] Twenty years later, the state was able to make an annual contribution of $150,000 to thirteen agricultural fairs from revenue generated at the Rock. In 1960, the fairs had actually lost $108,000. But the state's contribution, because of revenue received from the track, turned this loss into a profit.[51]

Smith delighted in playing an instrumental role in the viability of New Hampshire's agricultural community. He now had another ally every time the track's license came up for renewal before the General Court. In addition, the state benefited by keeping farmers financially solvent, but as a bonus, it gave Granite Staters another outlet to escape the harsh realities of life.

1933: A Salem landmark

1962: New lobby, Grandstand

1939: Smith's first remodeling

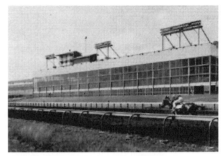

1962: New glass enclosed area

1955: Million dollar clubhouse added

1962: New mezzanine

The Rock's evolution: 1939-1962.

In 1937, Rockingham Park had paid $329,535.19 in overall wages, kicked in $612,910.21 in tax revenue, and gave another $37,000 to New Hampshire charities. One flyer distributed by the Rock boasted that "since the population of New Hampshire is 465,293 people, according to the latest United States Census, this sum is equal to $5.22 for every man, woman and child residing in the state."[52] Four years after operating as a legal gambling track, the Rock added $2.5 million to the state's treasury.[53]

The biennial state budget reached $17,000,000 in 1941.[54] Tax revenue from the track for that year and the following year exceeded $1,900,000.[55] This revenue source constituted more than 11 percent of the biennial state budget. About seven months before the Japanese attack on Pearl Harbor, New Hamp-

FACTS ABOUT ROCKINGHAM PARK THAT YOU AS A NEW HAMPSHIRE TAXPAYER SHOULD KNOW

$5.22 for every man for every woman for every child residing in the State of New Hampshire has been paid in TAXES by Rockingham Park

Rockingham Park has paid $2,432,674.99 in Taxes to the State of New Hampshire.

Since the population of New Hampshire is 465,293 people, according to the latest United States Census, this sum is equal to $5.22 for every man, woman and child residing in the state.

This total amount, $2,432,674.99 has been applied against the New Hampshire's State debt.

Where does this money come from? Almost entirely from out of state.

Figures show that:

    551,000 people have come to Rockingham Park by train from Boston.

    84.2% of the automobiles parked at Rocking-ham were cars with out-of-state licenses. This figure is based on 5 traffic counts made by the New Hampshire State Wide Highway Planning Survey.

Look at the record of Rockingham Park *for one year only*—the year 1937.

Taxes	$612,910.21
N. H. State Charities	37,000.00
Wages	329,535.19
1937 Total	$979,445.40

The fact is that since its opening in 1933 Rockingham Park has brought hundreds of thousands of people and millions of dollars into New Hampshire from out of state. Rockingham Park is a New Hampshire asset.

ROCKINGHAM PARK
SALEM, NEW HAMPSHIRE

In tough economic times the Rock contributed substantially to New Hampshire's coffers, as illustrated by this promotional fact sheet.

shire experienced one of its perennial "fiscal crises." Estimates placed the deficit between $500,000 and $1,000,000.

    Public policy makers, as they often would over the next several decades, turned to the track to help boost revenue.[56]

One month after news circulated that the state was faced with a roughly 6 percent deficit, the General Court voted to extend the Rock's gambling license for another two years.[57] An editorial in the *Manchester Union* observed: "... the state finds itself in absolute need of this money [tax revenue from Rockingham Park] to carry on its ordinary operations. The probable receipts are carefully estimated and included in the state budget as foreordained income over a considerable period ... An enterprise of whose legitimacy the people at large were doubtful only eight years ago has become a foundation stone for the solvency of the state treasury."[58]

Not surprisingly, the Rock's success caused numerous gambling bills to be introduced over the years ranging from Beano, to a statewide lottery, to the legalization of "betting establishments."[59] But the track's political influence in New Hampshire made sure it retained its gambling monopoly.

In 1955, 62 percent of the state's regular operating revenue came from "sin taxes" on beer, liquor, tobacco, and horse racing. These four sources furnished $10,450,000 of revenue. Liquor generated $4 million, cigarette and tobacco products kicked in $2.8 million, and Rockingham Park produced another $2.6 million for the treasury.[60] Two years later, according to an article in the *Concord Monitor and New Hampshire Patriot*, "the track gave the state $3,618,000 in revenue ... or nearly 20 per cent of all its general fund tax income."[61]

Because of the popularity and financial windfall to the state from thoroughbred racing, the introduction of night harness racing at Rockingham Park in 1958 seemed the logical next step. "The state government's solvency took another dip," wrote Leon Anderson in the *Monitor*, " when the Governor and Council dug into 'funds not otherwise appropriated' ... But taxpayers should not lie awake worrying about a general fund deficit. For Rockingham racetrack is set to give us some $600,000 from night harness racing this year ..."[62]

In its first year, night harness racing generated $565,509 for the state treasury. Tax revenue from thoroughbred racing brought in another $3 million. In 1958, 19.28 percent of the General Fund Budget Appropriations came from Rockingham Park.

One year after the introduction of harness racing, the *Boston Herald* observed that the General Fund budget provided for spending "of a record $76 million in the next two fiscal years ... but [Governor Powell] has emphasized that he has estimated $2.2 million of revenue from ... racing ..."[63] The total tax revenue from the Rock exceeded $4.1 million in 1960.[64]

Lane Dwinell, former New Hampshire House Speaker, Senate President, and governor, commented in 1996, "During my time in state government, the pari-mutuel tax was a very significant part of our revenue. But of course our budget was much less in those days than it is today. I recall raising the pari-mutuel tax to balance one of my budgets."[65]

The state's growing dependence on gambling could always be rationalized due to one overriding fact: the vast majority of bettors and thoroughbred

Judge George Grinnell of the Racing Commission (left), Governor Lane Dwin-nell (center), Bob Allard of the Racing Commission (right).

enthusiasts were not from New Hampshire. In 1937, more than 84 percent of the vehicles parked at Rockingham were from out-of-state. Approximately a half million people were from the Boston area.[66] Nineteen years later, 92 percent of all gamblers were from Massachusetts.[67] And in 1961, less than 10 percent of the $4.7 million the state received in tax revenue from the Rock came from New Hampshire residents.[68]

Professor Sam Rosen, of the University of New Hampshire, told three hundred municipal finance executives at a convention in 1967, "My state could not exist in comfort without encouraging the sins of our neighbors in obliging Massachusetts."[69] Professor Rosen continued: "Our expressways from the Massachusetts border to Rockingham Park show the greatest consideration for the comfort and well-being of Massachusetts bettors, without whom Rockingham could not exist and without whom our state government would not realize $7.5 million per year that comes from pari-mutuel taxes . . . New Hampshire has long depended more on gambling revenue than any other state in the Union, including Nevada, which depends more on a general sales tax."[70]

12/24/98

Gunther —

This may seem like an odd
book to give to you, and not
Kathy, especially in sight of
the title (ha ha). But I
read a chapter except in
historical Nutt — a periodical
of scholastic writings — and
was astanded by what I
read. I haven't read this
entire book, and by the
cover flaps am curious about
the motive of the book. Nonetheless,
the info provided regarding the
impact of gambling on the tax
structure of this state is
fascinating and something
I thought might interest
you as well. I give in appreciation
of your unstinting research
re: education in Nutt and the
forces that impact its quality.

merry Christmas! love Kathye with family

Not unlike today, the Granite State still relies on outsiders for tourism and sin tax dollars primarily from liquor and tobacco. And just as in decades of long ago, the state still faces regular budget shortfalls. As noted earlier, public policy makers debated the manner in which New Hampshire raised its revenue and the merit of a broadbased tax as early as 1927.

Gov. Lane Dwinell reflected that "one of the reasons [Rockingham Park] was so successful" stemmed from its proximity to Boston. "At that time we were living off our neighbors. We were exporting 60 percent of our liquor and more than half of our cigarettes. And at least 80 percent of the track's revenue came from outside the state. It's a historical fact, but I don't know if it's anything we should be proud of."[71]

"One of the interesting things," added Governor Dwinell, "is that New Hampshire is a pretty conservative state. We used to say that we were sensitive to living off sin. Racing, liquor, and tobacco were all sinful activities, and when 60 percent of the state's revenue came from those sources, we were happy, but we also blushed about it."[72]

The slightest hint that New Hampshire should consider a broadbased tax quickly brought the scorn of William Loeb of the *Union Leader*. The publisher and editorial page writer often pointed to the Rock as the solution: "Hysterical people who insist that we must have a broadbased tax (i.e., a sales tax) or any other new taxes should watch carefully to see whether [a substantial surplus in the state treasury materializes]. Besides, there is always the additional $300,000 that could be produced by adding an additional one per cent tax on the Rockingham racetrack, thus bringing New Hampshire's percentage up to the average which every other New England state taxes tracks."[73]

Usually, Lou Smith managed to dissuade the General Court from hiking the state's take. This caused a great deal of wrath from Loeb, who called it the "Rockingham Park lobbying scandal."

In the late 1950s, Governor Powell pursued "streamlining of state departments" and lawmakers began to seriously consider expanded forms of gambling to keep the state's financial house in order.[74] In 1962, Governor-elect John King, having taken a *no broadbased tax pledge* during the campaign, grappled with property taxes "zooming like a rocket," as one newspaper put it. In a sixteen year period, property taxes had gone up 258%.[75]

An editorial in the *Berlin Reporter* warned: "Unless there is a drastic reduction in costs of government on both the state and local level and unless there is a curtailment of services, there will be a need for new sources of income. So-called 'sin-taxes' and property taxes cannot continue to take care of the rising costs of government and of education . . . New taxes are not popular, but neither is the ever-rising property tax . . ."[76]

Gov. Walter Peterson resolved this issue by supporting a major overhaul of

Governor and Mrs. Wesley Powell.

the tax structure through the Business Profits Tax (BPT). "The Business Profits Tax," according to Governor Peterson, "became the single biggest source of revenue in the state government."[77]

In 1970, Governor Peterson called for a special session of the General Court. The BPT repealed and replaced the "municipal property tax on stock in trade, farm livestock and poultry, fuel pumps, and mills and machinery,"[78] wrote Leon Anderson in a history of New Hampshire's legislature. Not until Peterson left office, however, did this revenue source begin to make an impact on the state treasury. Eventually, the BPT generated substantial revenue, which reduced the state's reliance on Rockingham Park.[79]

In 1968, a year before the death of "the portly patriarch of our state government,"[80] as Smith was affectionately called by a journalist, Gov. John W. King issued a special proclamation recognizing Smith not just for his philanthropic contributions, but, just as importantly, also for the positive impact he had on the state's economy.[81] Proclamations are issued to celebrate many things, but recognizing the wealth generated for a state and its citizens by an individual is certainly unusual.

Governor and Mrs. King with Lou Smith.

One irate Massachusetts pundit reflected twenty-three years after Smith established his Salem track: "He's still [in Salem] and, after all these years, he's still the biggest news in New England racing. Weep for the past, my friends! Cry for the forgotten years when renegade politicians drove him out of Boston and forced him to settle in Salem Depot! Had he founded a racetrack here, this would be the race center of the United States today, and that's one of the prices a community must pay when its politicians are thieves."[82]

"The track was the main thrust for not getting a broadbased tax," recalls Rockingham County Commissioner and former state representative Ernie Barka. "No doubt about it. The fact that Massachusetts had every tax you could think of and they were still in trouble—people would cite that and then look at the revenue from racing here."[83]

Generating tens of millions of dollars for state coffers, with its rippling effect throughout the central-southern New Hampshire economy, gave Lou Smith an enormous amount of power. Although Smith did not actively seek that power, the Rock's mere existence gave it to him.

Lou Smith, second from left, U.S. Senator Thomas McIntyre, fourth from left behind jockey, and Gov. King at the end.

CHAPTER 3

Political Clout of Rock Founder
Lou Smith

U.S. senators, big city mayors, executive councilors, county sheriffs, governors, businessmen, and religious leaders all courted Lou Smith. Many revered him, others respected his entrepreneurial ability. People admired his talent to launch public relations campaigns to galvanize support. Many were concerned that his prowess could end a political career in the most subtle manner. Entrepreneurs sought his blessing for the success of a new business. Others were awed when in the blink of an eye Lou Smith took one of New Hampshire's many charities from insolvency to financial security with his legendary generosity. In a quiet, sometimes crusty manner, Lou Smith exuded power.

His testimony before the legislative committee considering the pari-mutuel bill in 1933 is one example of his skill as a political operative. Smith's influence did not derive just from the track, but also from his own individual ability. He seemed a master at understanding human nature. His involvement with getting the pari-mutuel bill passed in the General Court demonstrated an intuitive political skill. The nationally known writer Damon Runyon, a New York City sports reporter, wrote of Smith's appearance before a legislative committee of the General Court:

> He went there alone, with no political connections of any kind, and in a simple and direct manner he told the political leaders of the state that if they would permit him to operate racing at Rockingham Park, he was confident that he would return a considerable revenue to the state treasury in taxes.
>
> Here was a man whose methods were so open and above board they were almost bewildering.
>
> The racing bill went through both houses of the legislature with astonishing speed . . .
>
> And it did not cost Lou Smith a dime over and above his traveling and living expenses. Not one dime.[84]

Lutza Smith with U.S. Senator and Mrs. Edward Brooke (R-Mass.).

This is an understatement. The full story of how the bill passed the legislature with little opposition will probably never be fully known. Political deals that may have been cut behind closed doors in an era where such approaches in government were common will remain among the untold secrets of the State House.

Although the Great Depression clearly had an impact, Smith also knew how to manipulate the political environment. Damon Runyon, a friend of Smith's, proved a master at packaging. The renowned sportswriter wrote regularly about Lou Smith's integrity, character, and his ability to run "clean" tracks.[85] He helped to publicize, if not create, the persona and mystique of Lou Smith not just in New Hampshire but throughout the country as well.

In addition to the loyalty of men like Runyon, Smith surrounded himself with people of stature in the community. During his efforts to get the pari-mutuel bill passed, Smith asked Sam Simon, a concessionaire for Boston Garden and later Rockingham Park, for assistance in lobbying legislators. New Hampshire lawmakers knew of Simon before Smith's pari-mutuel bill ever came before the General Court.[86] Smith also retained two law firms to assist in getting the bill passed. One firm had a Democratic political pedigree and the

Gov. King, Mrs. Smith, and Mrs. King.

Richard 'Mac' O'Dowd, Hillsborough County Sheriff and later general manager of the Rock.

other, Republican.[87] Simon and the lawyers proved invaluable insiders, skillfully working the halls of power.

Smith also aggressively sought the loyalty of his detractors. The Rock offered jobs to many unemployed Rockingham County voters during one of the worst economic depressions ever faced by New Hampshire or the nation. This spurred business growth. Not surprisingly, Smith's track easily won the hearts and minds of the populace in Rockingham County.

In 1931, for example, Richard "Mac" O'Dowd, then Democratic sheriff of Hillsborough County, was directed by a Superior Court order, issued at the request of County Atty. George Scammon, to close Smith's track when it first opened. At the time, pari-mutuel gambling remained outlawed. O'Dowd had been asked to serve the court's order in light of the track's popularity and the awkward situation it would create for Rockingham County Sheriff Spinney.[88] No doubt Sheriff Spinney, up for reelection every two years, never overlooked the track's popularity among his voters.

Two years after gambling became legal, O'Dowd served as chief inspector for the New Hampshire State Racing Commission. Smith quickly befriended

O'Dowd and won his trust. In 1935, O'Dowd became the state director of personnel at the track, ensuring that Granite Staters received most of the jobs. Nine years later, he moved from the state payroll to become vice president and secretary of the New Hampshire Jockey Club. O'Dowd also worked as the Rock's treasurer and general manager.[89] He became legendary in the racing community and within New Hampshire in this latter position.

In 1961, at a testimonial dinner for O'Dowd, Bill Stearns said of him, ". . . the first time [O'Dowd] met Lou Smith at Rockingham Park was for the avowed purpose of putting a padlock on the joint. Mr. Smith, in turn, was so attracted by the genial young Irishman who came to arrest him that he put him to work as his right hand man . . ."[90]

John A. Green, another county official, served as president of the New Hampshire Jockey Club. Green was not just the Rockingham County Register of Deeds; he was also the "political boss of all Rockingham County,"[91] as one newspaper article termed him. He had a "political empire," said another article, ". . . and his influence, combined with the important Republican majority in Rockingham County, is largely responsible for the power of the track."[92]

In the late 1940s, Archbishop Richard J. Cushing, later cardinal, gave his public and enthusiastic support to Rockingham Park. In sharp contrast to Cushing, a frequent guest in the Smith home (an apartment overlooking the track), every other religious organization vehemently opposed the track. Cushing continued his support of it until his death. The Catholic leader not only accepted the philanthropy of Lou and his wife, Lutza, but he even celebrated an annual Mass on the track's field just before the start of a charity event for disabled children sponsored by a Catholic-operated hospital in the Boston area.

Two of the Granite State's top lawyers, Kenneth F. Graf and William Phinney were also closely linked to the track, until well after Smith's death in 1969. Graf served as president of the New Hampshire Jockey Association, and Phinney, as did Graf, looked out for its legal interests. Graf also had a sterling Republican pedigree.[93] Graf succeeded Smith, upon his death, as head of the track.

Phinney later temporarily severed his ties with the track, at least officially, to become the state attorney general in 1949. He continued to be affiliated with the law firm of Sheehan, Phinney & Bass. The latter name on the firm's marquee was for Perkins Bass, of Peterborough, former state Senate President, three term congressman, and father of current Congressman Charles Bass.[94] In 1955, the White House selected Phinney to serve as general counsel to the U.S. Defense Department.[95] Directly or indirectly, Lou Smith had access to anyone who could promote and protect the Rock.

Like a government without civil service safeguards, Smith operated Rockingham Park very much as a patronage driven bureaucracy reminiscent of Tam-

Cardinal Richard J. Cushing with Lutza Smith during a charity event at Rockingham Park

many Hall in New York City and James Michael Curley's Boston. William Barron, chair of Salem's selectmen, for example, used his position at the track to "judiciously" dole out 125 part-time and full-time jobs annually. In 1938, he purportedly gave out large sums of cash to needy families. He became "a candidate for the legislature, without opposition,"[96] according to the *New Hampshire Sunday News*.

The track figured prominently in many elections. Before state elections, often the track would formally invite all candidates for the state legislature to visit the Rock before it closed for the season. Harry T. Hayes, resident manager, told the candidates, ". . . we hope that our adversaries will not ask you to commit yourself against us until you are in possession of the facts."[97]

The Rock had an impact especially on the Republican Gubernatorial Primary involving Gov. Francis P. Murphy and Atty. Gen. Thomas P. Cheney in 1938. The attorney general said of his opponent: "No man can challenge my right to speak the truth. That is why I have not hesitated to strip the tinsel from the many false claims of the opposition camp. The most recent claim they make is that my opponent never had any interest in or connection with the Salem

Kenneth Folsom Graf. Lou Smith chose Graf's firm as legal counsel for Rocking-ham Park in 1933, the year pari-mutuel racing was introduced in New England.

racetrack. The claim is untrue. I know that he loaned that outfit $100,000 as recently as 1936."[98]

Smith also kept large sums of money in the Nashua Trust Company, of which Governor Frances P. Murphy served as vice president. But Smith insisted, like a Cheshire cat denying that he would cause trouble, "I have tried to keep out of politics," and noted that the track also had money in First National Bank of

CELEBRITIES AT ROCKINGHAM YESTERDAY. L. TO R., ROMA PEARSE, M RS. LOU SMITH, MARY CURLEY, LORETTA BREMNER, MRS. EMIL FUCHS, MRS. CHARLES GURGINHER, JUDGE FUCHS, AND MAYOR CURLEY.

Newspapers reported on prominent citizens of the day attending the Rock. Lutza Smith, second from left, and Mayor James Michael Curley on far right.

Boston.[99] Not long thereafter, the Nashua Trust Company lost the track's account.[100] Cheney, despite some accuracy to his charges, lost the election.[101]

The attorney general earned the wrath of track officials for trying to limit their profit and the displeasure of hundreds of employees and their families because jobs could be lost. He challenged the Rock's policy of keeping "breakage," or the odd sum over the "dime" in payoffs. Although extremely resistant to sharing the breakage, Smith reluctantly agreed with a legal opinion of the attorney general to hand over all breakage.[102] But soon thereafter, the state and the track agreed to split the breakage evenly. By 1962 breakage reached $500,000, of which the track and state still shared equally. Breakage had become the lifeblood for the Rock. But for breakage, the track would not have turned a $200,000 profit that year.[103]

Despite Cheney's electoral loss and the setback for gambling opponents, a few members of the General Court called for an investigation. But again their efforts were stymied. Regardless of charges that lawmakers were receiving bribes to support the Rock's interests, the House Ways and Means Committee voted unanimously to kill a bill that would have investigated the Salem track.[104] In 1938, the Hatcher Report, written and researched by Harold O. Hatcher at the request of the New Hampshire Congregational Church, alleged that in one year alone more than $100,000 had been paid out for "good will."[105]

Ironically, part of the track's power stemmed from the clout given to it, perhaps unknowingly, by the state. The Hatcher Report charged that the New Hampshire Racing Commission, established by the state to oversee the Rock, is "more active in defending racetrack operators than in protecting the public." It also said that because of the special treatment accorded to legislators, they "appear to be more in favor of the racetrack than any other single group in the state."[106] In short, the Rock's power fed on itself. Those mandated to supervise the happenings at the track indirectly received a paycheck by virtue of its existence.

In 1940, of the twenty-seven names submitted to the governor and Executive Council for consideration to serve on the State Racing Commission, four were directly connected to the General Court: Sen. A.A. Noel of Nashua and Reps. Leonard B. Peaver of Salem Depot, Richard G. Pray of Portsmouth, and Charles R. Thomas of Dublin. At the time, Atty. William Phinney, a close friend of Lou Smith's, served as chairman of the commission.[107]

Because of the commission's power, appointments to it were coveted. In 1956, U.S. Sen. Norris Cotton pushed for the appointment of Robert E. Allard to the Racing Commission. Allard, popular with the Franco-American community, a stronghold of Catholicism in Manchester which no doubt looked on Cardinal Cushing's visits to the Rock with interest, had solid credentials as a grassroots organizer. In 1954, Allard had supported Wesley Powell in an unsuccessful bid for the U.S. Senate against Cotton. A few political pundits have stated that without the candidacy of Robert Upton, Powell could have won. Speculation that Powell would run against Cotton prompted him to secure for Allard a commissioner's position in exchange for Allard's loyalty and help with the important Franco-American community.[108]

From an administrative standpoint, the commission maintained records on everyone who owned shares in Rockingham Park.[109] It also oversaw how the track collected pari-mutuel bets. The commission, with three members, promulgated regulations and issued the license that permitted the New Hampshire Jockey Club to conduct races at the Rock. With two permanent employees and twenty-seven temporary workers for the harness and thoroughbred meets, the commission maintained daily records of bets and the state's daily share.[110] Overall, the commission also played an important role in keeping out organized crime.

In 1955, Smith helped to organize a testimonial dinner for William Barron, former Salem selectman, superintendent of police, and comptroller of the New Hampshire Jockey Club. The event again demonstrated the political muscle of Lou Smith. More than 1,500 people turned out at the Rockingham Park Club House, including four former governors—Robert O. Blood, Charles M. Dale, Hugh Gregg, and Lane Dwinell. U.S. Senators H. Styles Bridges and Norris Cotton were in attendance, as were Congressman Chester Merrow, Atty. Gen.

Rockingham County political boss William Barron.

Louis Wyman, and Brig. Gen. Walter Arnold of Pease Air Force Base. Executive Councilors and throngs of local officials also paid tribute to one of the Rock's key employees. Justice Stephen M. Wheeler, of the New Hampshire Supreme Court, served as toastmaster.[111]

"If one was invited to a party down at the track," recalled Alan Pope, "then you had made it socially. It was the place where people of influence gathered. I'm sure I would have never been invited had it not been for the fact that I was administrative assistant [chief of staff] to the governors."[112]

Not surprisingly, the track became a popular stop for state and national politicians. In 1956, as one of many examples, the annual meeting of New Hampshire's mayors and city managers took a break from their work to visit the Rock.[113] Two years later, E.C. Ferguson and Wesley Powell, both competing for the Republican gubernatorial nomination, made an appearance at Lou Smith's open house inaugurating the harness racing season.[114]

Presidential candidates also found their way to the track. In reply to the question of what "presidential aspirants see in" the track, the *New Bedford Standard-Times* in Massachusetts answered, "more than 16 percent of [New Hampshire's] general fund revenues come [from] . . . one thoroughbred racing track . . ."[115] Candidates recognized Lou Smith's stature in the small state whose national importance was growing for being the first to vote in the presidential primary.

In 1949, Smith even had the power to bring the New Hampshire General Court to a standstill. The *Boston Herald* reported: "[The] decision to bring [the legislative session] to a temporary halt came abruptly this week as the cumbersome 400-member House was stalemated over the finance triangle . . . Another [reason] is the opening of the New Hampshire horse racing season next month, since some 40 lawmakers are employed as officials and clerks at the Rockingham Park racetrack."[116]

The *Christian Science Monitor* reported that among the Rock's stockholders were fourteen legislators, two executive councilors, and several state and county officials.[117] In the 1960s, due in part to the efforts of Stewart Lamprey, the names of Rockingham Park stockholders were made public.[118]

In 1955, Gov. Lane Dwinell, fully appreciating the political reality at the time, discounted any influence that the track might possess. "As for the track exercising control over the legislature," the governor said then, "I feel that is not true. Some members work for the track, and some own stock, and it is a matter of their own conscience."[119]

Once out of office, however, Governor Dwinell had a different recollection.

"[Lou Smith and track officials] were particularly interested in the Ways and Means Committee," remembered the former governor. "That's one of the reasons why I got to be chairman of the Ways and Means Committee. The [House] Speaker at the time wanted to have someone chair that committee who had never seen a horse. It was in their [New Hampshire Jockey Club's] best interest to have friends on that committee. Over the years, through [their] persistent lobbying of Speakers, they had a strong presence. It was felt [by the Speaker that] a person like myself [who] never had any connections with the track"[120] would bring some impartiality to the committee.

Still Governor Dwinell noted, "Even though they had influence, they didn't control the legislature. It's pretty hard to control over four hundred members."[121] Sen. Stewart Lamprey agreed: "Their influence over the state was exaggerated. They were interested in the problems that dealt with pari-mutuel betting."[122]

Lou Smith's clout in the General Court "always bothered me," said former Gov. Hugh Gregg. "It bothered the hell out of me. They were smart. That's where his bread was buttered." Despite Smith's power over the legislature, it "was all aboveboard. [Many] lawmakers worked over there. I understood all that. There was nothing illegal about that. It was just smart business practice. And I accepted it that way,"[123]

"[Rockingham Park] had a tremendous impact [on New Hampshire]," added Governor Gregg. "We would have been in deep trouble [without the track]. We would have had to pass a new tax. That's why we didn't object when they brought up bills in the legislature and [many] legislators were working over there."[124]

Former New Hampshire House Speaker and Gov. Walter Peterson reflected that Lou Smith "was one of the people you had to see and treat with respect." After Peterson decided to run for House Speaker in the late 1960s, he made a visit to the track: "It was an important courtesy call you had to make. And it was important that you handled it right." Smith "had quite a lot of influence in the legislature," he said.[125]

Lou Smith never publicly endorsed candidates, but he did give his unofficial blessing by escorting office seekers through the track. "The best thing that could happen to a candidate in those days," recalled Governor Dwinell, "was to get Lou Smith to take you around the ticket sellers or cashiers. A lot of them were legislators, and if they saw you with Lou Smith, it subtly indicated that the track wasn't against you."[126]

In addition, thousands of patrons would see Smith with the candidate of choice. In 1934, for example, attendance exceeded 490,000, for a daily average of 7,963. In 1946, almost 900,000 war-weary people attended races at the Rock, for a daily average of 13,041. In 1964, attendance reached 934,000 for thoroughbred racing, which translated into a daily average of 15,568.[127] The Rock was always a great place for a politician to campaign.

Not long before the official entry of the United States into World War II, about thirty members of the General Court were drawing salaries from Rockingham Park. At one point, Governor Dwinell recalled, "We figured that seventy-five members of the House of Representatives worked for the track. Even more than that would drink the racetrack's free liquor over at the Eagle Hotel [in Concord] after sessions."[128]

Stewart Lamprey, however, successfully beat the track at its own game. During his run for House Speaker in 1958, he galvanized support by promising to diminish, at least during his tenure, the power of Rockingham Park. Not only did he beat the track's candidate, Rep. Sam Green, but he also cleared out many of the state employees "placed" in the legislature by the Rock.

"They had their candidate—Sam Green," he recalled. "Sam Green was a wonderful man. I thought a lot of Sam and still do. But he was a track man. It was a good, hard-fought fight over principles. They were fighting for their principles. I was fighting for mine. They did it aboveboard. And I did it aboveboard too," said Lamprey. "I was out to diminish the influence of the track in the legislature. I never made any bones about it.[129]

"I never went to see Lou Smith [referring to the obligatory courtesy call]," adds Lamprey. "I got into my automobile and saw all the legislators. I spent a full sixty days on the road seeing the legislators and telling them my story of why I should be elected Speaker. And the track was a big part of it."[130]

Atty. Robert A. Shaines, lobbyist for the Seabrook greyhound track that battled Smith's attempts to stop the expansion of gambling in the 1950s, observed that "the racing industry, generally, lives or dies by its affinity with the legislatures of the various states. They determine the breakage [percentage of revenue] that can be taken by the track. When your economic ability to make money or not depends on the goodwill of the legislature—I dare say that every track in the country has a very heavy legislative lobby program. They [track owners] wine and dine and are very cordial to the people they need to be [wooing]."[131]

Due to the Rock's access to the State House, a law was passed prohibiting state legislators from working at the track during a session of the General Court. This would limit any conflict of interest. Because race meets rarely if ever, overlapped with a legislative session, this law had little impact.[132] Within five years of opening, the track also employed the chairman of the Salem Board of Selectmen and then Gov. Francis P. Murphy's brother.[133] In 1955, the Rock had 793 employees and in 1967,[134] two years before Lou Smith's death, it had 650 people[135] on its payroll—all, along with their families, potential voters.

Stewart Lamprey has a pragmatic outlook on the presence Smith had in the State House. "Since the beginning of the country there has always been influential parties in the legislative process," he said. "Lou Smith wanted to protect his interest, and like any good businessman," he achieved his aim within the bounds of the law. But the senator is quick to add that there must always be a check on such power. Referring to the challenge he launched against the track, he reflected, "Some people have to stand up and be counted. It's very important."[136]

Mike Dagostino recalled that the son and brother of Sam Cohen, sports editor for the *Boston Record American,* had a job at the track. "In those days," said Dagostino, "you did the right thing. You took care of your people. You took care of your friends. Everything was aboveboard. Everybody helped one another."[137] Not surprisingly, the Rock always had favorable coverage in the sports pages. This only furthered Smith's stature and mystique as a powerful player on the political landscape.

Rockingham Park even had the influence to block a move by the New England Patriots into New Hampshire. "We came very close to getting the New England Patriots in Salem" in the late 1960s, recalled Governor Peterson. "Foxborough won out. We were going to build a stadium across the street from Rockingham Park. It was a pretty near thing. The racetrack people, behind closed doors . . . scuttled it. It would have competed with their interests."[138]

As briefly discussed earlier, the Rock's power did eventually diminish, due, in part, to Governor Peterson's restructuring of the state's tax base. Revenue growth "had been maximized from the track," said Peterson, and hence new sources were needed. The stock and trade tax added to these fiscal constraints.

Under the old tax structure, material in warehouses could be taxed. "Machinery was taxed before it actually produced," observed Peterson. "That was changed to the profit made from the activity. The effect was to open the state to considerable expansion of economic activity."[139] And with this expansion of economic activity, coupled with the work of Stewart Lamprey, came the diminishment, during the 1970s, of the Rock's political power.

CHAPTER 4

The Great Political Wars

The allowance and eventual expansion of legalized gambling by the state government tore at New Hampshire's soul. It became one of the most divisive, controversial, and prolonged issues Granite Staters had to confront in the twentieth century. Critics charged, as discussed in the previous chapter, that the track influenced elections and controlled votes in the General Court.

During the Great Depression, most Christian organizations, with the exception of the Catholic Church, banded together to fight renewal of the track's gambling license. Twenty years later a spirited debate began over whether to permit gambling at a greyhound racetrack in nearby Seabrook and thus put an end to the Rock's monopoly. But Lou Smith's political alliances and his exceptional ability at creating the image that the Rock was synonymous with New Hampshire turned the tide. It also again underscored just how much power Smith wielded.

THE FIGHT AGAINST GAMBLING

In the late 1930s, Smith's payroll of political leaders proved its worth as Christian groups organized a tough campaign to end legalized gambling. On May 4, 1938, Rev. C. Austin Earle, moderator of the New Durham Baptist Association, fired one of the first rounds against the track, telling congregants at an annual meeting, "We are opposed to having our state a partner in commercial gambling and taking its share of the revenue."[140] About two weeks later, participants at the 137th annual meeting of the New Hampshire Congregationalist Church also voiced strong concerns about the state's growing dependence on the track. The Congregationalist Committee on Social Action reported that a "research worker" had been hired to gather information about the track.[141]

The Congregational Church published a thirty-four page article in its magazine *Social Action* confirming the suspicions of the Rock's detractors. The article, authored by New York investigator Harold O. Hatcher, charged that the Rock donated heavily to political campaigns, employed relatives of key political leaders, gave out free passes to all members of the General Court, and even had ties to New York's Tammany Hall boss James J. Hines.

At the time, Hines was indicted by Manhattan District Attorney, later three-term New York governor, Thomas E. Dewey. Former legal counsel to the track, Joseph Shalleck, was closely linked to Hines. This link, according to Hatcher, prompted the Manhattan District Attorney's Office to investigate the Hines-Rockingham connection. Smith, denying charges that he was under investigation by the notorious New York racketbuster, said, "If that were so, Dewey would be after me too,"[142] with a formal investigation or Grand Jury indictment.

The Manhattan District Attorney ultimately convicted the Tammany boss. And at sentencing the court learned, according to Hatcher, that Hines received a paycheck from the New Hampshire Breeders Association, a group started by Lou Smith. According to a probation report, "During the years 1931 to 1935 inclusive the only moneys earned by the defendant were received from the New Hampshire Breeders Association, an organization associated with the Rockingham Park race-track and for which Joseph Shalleck is attorney." In 1931, Hines was paid $3,300 and in the following two years $2,500. In 1934, the track paid him $6,300; $6,500, the following year.[143] As for Smith, no charges were ever brought against him.

Goodwill or not, Smith could not escape a legislative hearing on the relicensing of the track in 1939. The hearing in Concord, although not focused on specific allegations of corruption, did address the moral issue of gambling. There was a great deal at stake for religious leaders, as Smith was pushing for an eight-year renewal rather than the two or four year renewal. The same charges about gambling, ranging from the breakup of homes to the endangerment of youths, were made by Christian groups[144]. The hearing was one of the longest in the state's history.[145]

In 1939, the House Ways and Means Committee voted 19 to 4 in favor of renewing the track's gambling license for six years (in 1935 it had been renewed for four years) and nullified Attorney General Cheney's legal opinion regarding breakage. Rather than breaking to the penny, the track would break to ten cents. This meant a windfall of $90,000 to the track and the state.[146] The House of Representatives approved the bill by a 259 to 136 margin.[147]

The bill also provided for an increase in the state's take on bets, from 3.5 percent to 4 percent.[148] In the Senate, the bill passed with a 13 to 10 vote[149] with amendments increasing the state's take and renewing the track's license for four years.[150] The final version signed into law by the governor differed little from the Senate bill; the state's betting take increased to 4.5 percent.[151] Within two years of Smith's death, New Hampshire's share reached 14 percent.[152] As discussion began in the late 1950s to raise the rate to 16 percent, Atty. William Phinney

Ken Graf, left, with Bob DeStasio, racing secretary.

warned lawmakers, "It would kill the goose that lays the golden egg."[153] A twenty-five year audit conducted in 1961 found that the state received 39.1 percent of the track's gross revenue and its stockholders a mere 4.2 percent.[154]

Other concerns about legalized gambling stemmed from the professional criminals that it could attract. Due in large part to Smith's ability to keep tight control of his track, Rockingham flourished as a "clean" establishment in comparison to other tracks in the country.

According to Eddie Hurley, writing for the *Daily Record* in 1933: "Smith is flanked by one of the wisest race horse men in the country in Jim Munroe, the racing secretary, who also supervised the construction of the new plant while he brought in a set of racing officials whose reputations are unblemished and if the meeting has been marked by various disciplinary measures against jockeys and owners, it is simply because Smith will not stand for anything that in the least resembles the sinister."[155] In 1936, to keep out the "sinister" element, Smith founded the New Hampshire Jockey Club. Membership required owning its stock.

Because of similar concerns about organized crime owning any of the track's 350,000 shares of stock, the shareholders under Smith's management created a voting trust. Twelve hundred stockholders owned a piece of the Rock. Lou and Lutza owned 17,849 shares,[156] a controlling interest.

In 1956, at a stockholders meeting that renewed Lou Smith's ten year contract, three men were given control of the trust—Smith; Eugene L. Norton, a New York City attorney; and Richard M. O'Dowd, the former Hillsborough County Sheriff.[157] In this manner Smith kept out undesirable elements who might have sought influence or a controlling interest. As a result, "for more than 45 years," says a press release, "the Club has ensured the integrity of world-class horse racing at Rockingham Park."[158]

This is not to suggest that Smith didn't have problems. No doubt Smith learned some of the many hard lessons about life at an early age, having run away from home as a boy. As part owner of Rockingham Park, he even became the target of a kidnaping plot by Pasquale Longo, Louis Gambino, Nathan Stein, and Nicholas Merconti, all of Boston. These men were actually arrested by federal law enforcement officials for their involvement in a narcotics ring. According to William E. Clark, supervisor of the New England narcotics division, the four men had made plans to kidnap Lou Smith and extract a sizable ransom.[159]

Smith knew that his philanthropy earned him a great deal of goodwill. But he also understood that such generosity had its limitations. No amount of charity or public relations gimmicks would prevent the New Hampshire General Court from terminating the track's gambling license if illegal activity took root at the Rock.

"He was a very sharp businessman," recalled Governor Hugh Gregg. "He knew the value of a dollar and knew what he needed to do. And he knew the importance of having a good reputation in the state. He would have been killed if he hadn't [a good reputation]. If there is any state that is anti-gambling—we probably come as close to it as any state. And Lou knew it. He knew that he'd have to deal with churches and do-gooders. Reputation was important to him."[160]

In 1960, the track expelled Carmine Tamello of Providence, Rhode Island, and Danny Raimondi of Fall River, Massachusetts, two known bookies. Their conduct was, according to the judge who later heard the case, "inconsistent with the orderly and proper conduct of a race meeting."[161] The two men filed a lawsuit against the track and lost. The state Supreme Court observed, based on information from the track, that they had associated and consorted "with persons with known criminal records and who are not interested in furthering racing and pari-mutuel wagering on a sound and respectable basis."[162]

In addition to concerns about organized crime, detractors also insisted that the track would abandon New Hampshire, now very dependent on gambling revenue, should a better business environment be created in another state. Oth-

Lou Smith with Hugh Gregg, New Hampshire's youngest and most dapper governor.

ers complained that state leaders had lost political control to gambling inter-ests. In 1949, for example, the license was again up for renewal and Vernon L. Phillips, chair of the Congregational Conference for Social Action, charged that Rockingham Park had the state "by the [financial] throat." He added that the track "will forget about paying your charities and taxes and it will move out" should it no longer be profitable to operate in New Hampshire.[163]

Rev. W. M. Setzer, of the First Baptist Church of Manchester, said the Rock "lives on what the rest of us produce."[164] Despite widespread, vocal protests, the House of Representatives voted a gambling license extension by a 318 to 52 rollcall vote.[165] And the Senate subsequently agreed.

An editorial writer for the *Claremont Eagle* observed: "... shortly after the war [1945], when the track management was considering passing up a 'charity meet' of three or six days, there was such a deluge of pleadings for this type of aid from dozens of organizations, that ... some of the organizations went so far as to point out ... that they had come to plan their annual budget on this type of support."[166] As to a drug, charitable organizations became addicted to gambling.

Ironically, many of God's Christian soldiers accepted, while at the same time condemning, the charity of Rockingham Park. A few years later a minister observed, "One year the track will pay for the heating bill, another year for something else."[167] Even sermons against gambling did not stop or limit Smith's generosity. "They are very generous with everybody up there at Rockingham Park."[168] There was another reality—by 1949 the Rock paid $18 million to the state treasury[169] and again helped to stave off the imposition of a broadbased tax.

The gambling controversy raged from the 1930s until the 1950s. But through goodwill, public relations manipulation, and extending charity to critics, Lou Smith beat a very formidable coalition, one that included, at some time or another, Baptists,[170] Adventists,[171] Methodists,[172] Universalists,[173] Congregationalists,[174] the Christian Civic League,[175] the Council of Churches,[176] and Sunday school workers.[177] No doubt Smith saw the benefits of cultivating a public friendship with Cardinal Cushing of Boston, which neutralized Christian opposition and limited future opposition from religious leaders. What would normally have been a public relations fiasco for anyone else proved just a minor challenge to Smith.

EXPANDING GAMBLING

While most religious groups banded against the Rock to end its gambling license, they also joined with the track, in an unofficial capacity, to fight the issuance of a gambling license for greyhound dog racing. Stopping greyhound gambling, however, stemmed more from Lou Smith's business concerns than from any threat posed by religious leaders on moral grounds. After all, many religious leaders needed the Rock's charity to survive. According to Leon Anderson, of the *Monitor & New Hampshire Patriot*: "Rockingham Kennel Club made a big splurge before the 1955 legislature, by announcing that some 250 Granite Staters had subscribed $50,000 to finance an effort to win legalization of night dog racing as a new source of revenue to help balance state finances . . . For a brief period it appeared this concerted drive would win approval. But then Rockingham racetrack . . . swung into action and the House of Representatives voted against the dogs by a heavy majority."[178]

Lou Smith asserted publicly, "It's our experience that we can't profitably operate in competition with dogs. Even Massachusetts [dog] tracks have an adverse effect upon our operation."[179] Smith's concerns were well founded. On a rainy, summer Saturday in nearby Revere, for example, 17,726 people showed up at the dog track and wagered $538,057.[180]

Smith rarely commented publicly. It wasn't his style. He dominated the political and social scene without being ostentatious or even obvious, preferring to leave his savvy lawyers or lobbyists to act on his behalf. Hence, a few choice words by "Uncle Lou" for the newspapers about the negative impact on over-all state revenues would be especially noted throughout the hills and vales of New Hampshire.

Proponents of legal pari-mutuel dog racing argued that the Salem track didn't have a monopoly on gambling. In addition, Atty. Stanley M. Burns of Dover, spokesman for the Rockingham Kennel Club, estimated that another $1 million would be generated for the state if gambling occurred at greyhound facilities.[181] Atty. Robert A. Shaines of Portsmouth, counsel for the New Hampshire Greyhound Racing Association at the time, testified before a leg-islative committee in 1959. He told members of the General Court: "What could be fairer than our bill, which provides for local option in towns where a track would be located?"[182]

James C. Falconer, chairman of the Seabrook Board of Selectmen, told the committee that dog tracks could provide "much-needed tax relief" for localities. But State Rep. Ralph Sanborn, of Hampton Falls, cautioned that there might not be enough gambling dollars to go around. Atty. Richard E. Dill of Rye, repre-senting the Rye Bethany Congregational Church, cautioned that New Hampshire "by erosion is moving toward the standards of Nevada. Every step in that direc-tion is an unhappy step."[183] Ralph W. Smith, general manager of the Rockingham Kennel Club, called the Lou Smith-Christian coalition "an unholy alliance."[184]

Frank D. O'Neil, respected State House reporter for the *Union Leader*, wrote, "The sight of the Rockingham Park horse barons holding hands with so-called moral bloc leaders was something that made State House observers—at least this one—blink and wonder what crazy twist this gambling hassle will take next."[185] But then again, seeing Cardinal Cushing celebrate an annual Mass on the field of the Rock was also something to cause a person to "blink and wonder."

Atty. Shaines reflected, "My belief is that some of those groups [Christian organizations joining with the Rock to oppose greyhound racing] were stimu-lated by nice contributions. If you're going to come in to lobby for Rockingham Park by lobbying against competition . . . I need say no more."[186]

An editorial in the *News & New Boston Times* warned against expanding gambling: "And when gambling comes into the picture, so does big money. Corruption follows as surely as a Bill Loeb editorial against Communism. The spectacle of ministers and the horsey fraternity holding hands in a joint effort to kill dog racing at the recent hearing, only seems to prove that 'politics makes strange bedfellows.'"[187]

State Rep. Louis I. Martel, of Manchester, pleaded with his colleagues, including the 10 percent who were on the Rock's payroll, to "vote as your con-science tells you to vote, not according to what Lou Smith asked you to do, or paid you to do."[188]

In 1958, House Speaker W. Douglas Scammon said that in the debate over extending legalized gambling to a dog track, Rockingham Park held the "balance of power" on all such gambling issues. One Rock official even purportedly had the hubris to tell the House Speaker that "New Hampshire will legalize dog racing when we want it, and not before."[189]

Attorney Shaines stated, "We knew that Rockingham Park would be opposed to having a racing facility in Seabrook. The biggest obstacle was the tightness between members of the legislature and Rockingham Park. Lou Smith and Mac O'Dowd pulled in their notes with key people in the legislature who felt beholden to them. They made sure that they had a good, solid base in the legislature. That's tough to overcome. Everybody was a Lou Smith sympathizer. He was a very likable guy."[190]

"Cordiality of the opposition" is the Portsmouth attorney's greatest memory regarding his advocacy on behalf of the Seabrook dog track. "But [Lou Smith]," Shaines adds with respect for Smith's Machiavellian ways, "could afford to be cordial because he knew where his votes were."[191]

An editorial in the *Worcester Telegram & Gazette* noted: "The New Hampshire Legislature, to be sure, has previously taken a wholly righteous attitude about dog racing—but this came easy to a Legislature which includes 40 to 50 members who are on the Rockingham horse track payroll."[192]

"There's no question," observed Shaines, "that Lou Smith made a lot of friends where he needed to have a lot of friends."[193] Legalized greyhound gambling didn't come about until after Lou Smith's death.

Gov. Walter Peterson, who signed the bill legalizing gambling at the dog track in Seabrook, reflected, "Ken Graf [legal counsel for Rockingham Park] personally came up to argue the point" of vetoing the bill. "I listened, but I thought that it was one business trying to block a competitor. There was no great moral ground on which they could argue. The key issue was making sure things were run honestly."[194] In short, the issue came down to whether the Rock should have a monopoly on gambling.

By the late 1950s, debate raged over the introduction of a sweepstakes lottery. In 1959, Rep. George Gilman expressed concern that the state wouldn't just be permitting gambling, but would now be in the business of gambling. Rep. Ernest R. Coutermarsh argued that the governor's failure to support a sweepstakes lottery bill would equate to "killing Santa Claus." And Representative Wayne Crosby thought "we look like a lot of clowns to the rest of the country for even considering such a measure."[195]

On March 12, 1964, according to the New Hampshire Sweepstakes Commission, 198 of 211 New Hampshire communities began selling sweepstake tickets. "And so the story goes . . . Since New Hampshire initiated a lottery, 37 other states, along with the District of Columbia, Puerto Rico, the Virgin Islands, and five Canadian Provinces, have put lotteries into operation . . . Sales have gone from $5.7 million in 1964 to more than $176 million in 1997."[196] It

Gov. King buys the first sweepstakes ticket. Winners were determined by a race at the Rock and revenues benefitted education.

gave the Racing Commission authority to hold a sweepstakes on any horse race in the world.[197] Gov. John W. King said he signed the bill "at a time when our people are carrying a cross of taxation unequaled in American history."[198]

The New Hampshire Sweepstakes, vehemently opposed by the Christian Civic League, the Congregational Christian Conference, the New Hampshire Taxpayers Federation, and the League of Women Voters, was projected to raise about $2 million a year by designating two races each season at Rockingham Park as sweepstakes events.[199]

Thirty-six electronic sweepstakes ticket machines were set up at the Rock and two hundred at forty-nine state liquor outlets. Education benefited from the revenue generated.[200] Sweepstakes winners were determined by a race at the Rock.[201] In 1968, the state held a sweepstakes based on a harness race—a one mile "classic" for invited three year old pacers. The event, organized by the New Hampshire Trotting and Breeding Association at the Rock, with a $50,000 prize, was the largest purse in New England history.[202] And today, "every scratch ticket and lottery," says Salem historian Douglas Seed, "can be linked to New Hampshire's sweepstakes race."[203]

Gov. King with Miss NH Sweepstakes and Lou Smith.

But amid all the political shenanigans and debate about gambling as an appropriate means to raise revenue, Granite Staters were very proud of the Rock. It captured a certain glamour that changed New Hampshire's reputation as a gritty textile state that had fallen on hard times to an attractive tourist destination that offered the majesty of a fine sport coupled with a bit of Hollywood flair.

CHAPTER 5

A Nation in Need of Escape and Heroes

Hundreds of thousands of patrons flocked to the Salem track annually. "It was the only place to be," said Mike Dagostino, personnel manager, who ensured for the state that a certain percentage of New Hampshire residents were hired at the track.[204] "It was a festive place to go," recalled Louise Newman, secretary to Lou Smith.[205] Rockingham County Commissioner Ernie Barka reflected on the many occasions he spent at the track: "Those were happy times. It was a happy part of my life. They're good memories."[206]

On opening day, June 21, 1933, Lou Smith breathed life into Rockingham Park. Al Jolson[207] and Governor Ely of Massachusetts were expected to join some 15,000 patrons that day.[208] Forty police officers were hired to direct traffic and keep order.[209] Ironically, one of the men who worked tirelessly with Smith to see this day happen, Damon Runyon, "owner of a select stable of good horses, including Frigate Bird," as he was described in a newspaper article, did not participate in the day's festivities.[210]

The excitement ushered in on that June day only multiplied with each passing year. Lou Smith and his wife, Lutza, of Winnipeg, Canada, hobnobbed with Judy Garland,[211] Jack Dempsey,[212] Frank Sinatra, Jr.,[213] Mickey Rooney, Sammy Davis, Jr.,[214] James Michael Curley,[215] H. Styles Bridges,[216] Gov. Nelson Rockefeller,[217] and William and Nackey Loeb,[218] among others. Most of New Hampshire's chief executives would make at least one obligatory visit to present the governor's cup trophy at an annual race held in honor of the state's top politician.[219]

"I would go over with my wife several times a season," recalled Governor Gregg, "just to see what was going on. We always went to the restaurant for dinner. I love rice pudding. They found that out, and when I came over, they always had rice pudding for me. I never had such good rice pudding as in that restaurant. Good restaurant."[220]

Wilt Chamberlain, star player for the Philadelphia 76ers, and his coach

The Rock in the mid-1930s.

Alex Hannum made a pilgrimage to the nationally renowned track.[221] Larry MacPhail, former owner of the Brooklyn Dodgers and the New York Yankees, not only patronized the Rock, but also raced his thoroughbreds there.[222]

Even overseas the Rock had a following. Within hours of being presented to the Massachusetts General Court, His Serene Highness, Hans Adam, Crown Prince of Liechtenstein, was escorted to Salem.[223] Prince Hans, a horse enthusiast, knew well the Rock's reputation even in central Europe. He presented the trophy at the Liechtenstein Handicap before leaving for a meeting with President John F. Kennedy at the White House.[224]

In April 1969, famed Metropolitan Opera diva Eileen Farrell came to the track and presented a trophy for the $25,000 Romeo Hanover Pace.[225] Friends of the Smiths included Walter Winchell, Ruby Keeler, and movie studio giant Louis B. Mayer. Crowds at the Rock were in awe. Even the thoroughbred Savuesco attracted spectators, for reasons in addition to racing: Singer Bing Crosby owned the horse. Savuesco won three times in one season at the Rock.[226]

If Granite Staters weren't reading in local, regional, and national papers about the celebrities and political figures coming to the track, they read about the attendance of Lou or Lutza at a grand dinner. In 1962, Lou presented a rac-

Hans Adam, Crown Prince of Liechtenstein, with Lutza Smith.

ing award at the Annual B'nai B'rith Sportsmen Dinner in Boston. The folks back home read about Smith dining with Senator-elect Edward M. Kennedy, Red Sox manager Johnny Pesky, Red Sox first baseman Carl Yastrzemski, and boxer Cassius Clay (Muhammad Ali).[227]

The Smiths were often mentioned on the society pages of major newspapers. In 1951, people read about television celebrity Ed Sullivan making a personal request on behalf of the Smiths to some New York toy makers, the Marx brothers. The toy makers, at the request of Sullivan, provided twenty-three crates of toys to 106 disabled children at the Joseph P. Kennedy Jr. Memorial Hospital on Warren Street in Brighton.[228] On another occasion, New Englanders learned from the *Boston Record* that "Lou Smith, by the way, is looking for a carnival—a whole carnival—to stage a show on the grounds of the Kennedy Memorial Hospital."[229] Lou Smith became one of New England's favorite heroes.

The Smiths were affectionately called Uncle Lou and Auntie Lutza for their generosity to charities. Although childless, they often directed their philanthropy to children's causes. Beth Israel Hospital, Boston Children's Hospital, and Shriners Hospitals in Springfield and Philadelphia were among the recipients of their largesse.[230]

Jack Dempsey, world heavy weight champion, with Lutza Smith (probably in New York City).

In addition, Lou Smith often held a special charity day, on which he would donate much of the day's profits to a worthy cause. The Red Cross benefited from a special day in August 1955. New England had been hit hard that year by floods, and Lou Smith, never missing an opportunity to offer help, held a Red Cross Day at the Rock.[231] In 1969, Lou Smith held three charity days for the Gov. John Winant New Hampshire Tuberculosis Association. This charity received more than $40,000 that year.[232]

Rockingham County Commissioner Ernie Barka recalled raising money for the Jimmy Fund: "Smith allowed the group to have volunteers stand by the gates with buckets. We collected over $2,000 that day—then Lou Smith arranged to make it into a media event by getting Ted Williams involved."[233]

"No one," insisted Mike Dagostino, "did more for the nuns in New Hampshire than Lou Smith. My sister-in-law [a nun] went to Windham when she retired. They had a car that broke down and wouldn't pass inspection. Lou Smith told me to go to a car dealership and bring with me a dozen roses and a dollar bill." Dagostino gave the roses to the secretary and the dollar bill to the car dealer. "I got a beautiful Buick four-door Roadmaster for the nuns," he recalls.[234]

Lutza Smith, Cardinal Cushing, and Lou Smith on a holiday visit with disabled children.

The Rockingham Park Charity Foundation served as another vehicle for the distribution of charity. Trustees included Lou Smith, representatives from the Jewish and Christian faiths, and significant politicians, such as the governor and the attorney general.[235] New Hampshire Catholic Charities, New Hampshire Children's Aid Society, Daniel Webster Home for Children, Crotched Mountain Rehabilitation Center, and Friends of Young Judea were among the charities that benefited.[236]

The favorite charity of the Smiths, started by Lutza, was the Non-Sectarian Fund for Crippled Children. Cardinal Richard J. Cushing served as the group's honorary chairman. Adding to the Rock's glamour were Lutza's annual fund raising clambakes for disabled youngsters. Jerry Vale and Frankie Avalon performed at Lutza's annual charity event.[237] In 1949, the *Newburyport* (Massachusetts) *News* called Lutza's event the "most colorful social and charitable event in the history of American racing."[238]

The nation's top entertainers performed at the Frolics a nightclub at nearby Salisbury. Sammy Davis Jr., Andy Williams, Ella Fitzgerald, Johnny Mathis, Frankie Avalon, the McGuire Sisters, and Liberace were among the perform-

Lou Smith with band leader Tony Bruno, of Boston, one of many entertainers who appeared at the Rock.

ers during its 1960 season.[239] Not surprisingly, Lutza drew from this resource for entertainment at her clambakes. And even if the stars weren't available for a show at the Rock, it was a sure bet that the glitz and glamour of the entertainment world, when time permitted, would make their way to the Rock to watch a race.

"Lou Smith's connection to Cardinal Cushing," said County Commissioner Barka, "helped to get celebrities to make an appearance at the track. When Cardinal Cushing called, [entertainers] had to answer or they were going to hell. He promised them that. They didn't refuse a cardinal."[240]

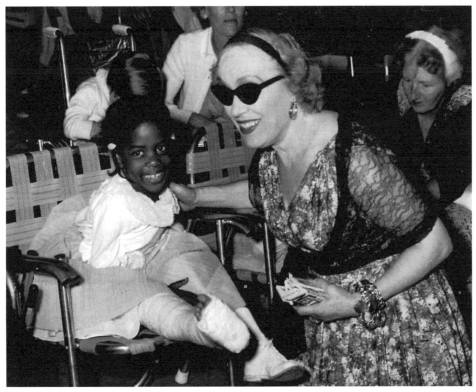

Lutza Smith with one of "God's sick angels."

During an interview in 1948, Lou and Lutza reminisced about their twenty-five years of marriage. "They had been good years," Lou Smith told the reporter. "They'd have been even better," Lou said, "with a couple of children around the house," Lutza nodded. The decision came shortly thereafter to help disabled children.[241] Lutza received a charter from the state of New Hampshire for the Crippled Children's Non-Sectarian Fund. John R. Macomber, of Framingham, donated five hundred shares of Rockingham Park stock to the fund and served as its first president.[242]

Lutza, dubbed the "finest dressed woman on the turf,"[243] by a Texas newspaper, called the needy children "God's sick angels."[244] Attendance at one of Auntie Lutza's events could easily exceed 3,000 people.[245] Louise Newman recalled a figure as high as 10,000.[246] "If you ran a horse there," recalled Mike Dagostino, "you had to buy a ticket. No one got into the clambake for free." Mrs. Smith could also be seen selling candy bars in the grandstand to raise additional money.[247]

Prior to the festivities, a Catholic Mass was celebrated at the track by a local priest with the assistance of Cardinal Cushing who always took the

Lutza sells chocolate to a patron.

opportunity to address the crowd.[248] In 1949, Cushing, then an Archbishop, told the thousands of guests assembled at the third annual clambake: "These children are entitled to more service than they receive from the state. In Massachusetts alone, we have 5,000 physically and mentally deficient children, whose parents go around to hospitals knocking at the door and asking for help. The doors do not open, for there is no room. The state has a responsibility for its children, but it perhaps is impossible, at this time . . . Thus personal and individual charities must maintain these institutions."[249]

As noted, Cushing's attendance also sent a clear message about his views on Rockingham Park. The Catholic War Veterans (CWV) sent an equally clear message in 1956, when they held their twenty-first Annual National Convention in Manchester and spent an afternoon watching the CWV Handicap at the Rock.[250]

In 1961, the Smiths donated the money to build a surgical wing at the Kennedy Hospital.[251] By 1969, Lou and Lutza had raised and donated over $2 million to help disabled children.[252] This generosity continued well after their passing with the establishment of the Lou and Lutza Smith Foundation.

Wedding anniversary of the Smiths in 1961 celebrated at the Kennedy Hospital.

If Lutza wasn't fussing over the annual clambake, she was planning one of her many children's parties. Thanksgiving, Christmas, Mother's Day, Father's Day, the Smiths' anniversary, even their birthdays were a treat for disabled youngsters, with parties on each of these occasions.[253] On Mother's Day in 1956, Lutza not only brought presents for the children at Kennedy Memorial Hospital, but she treated the youngsters to pony rides as well.[254] Over 2,800 children benefited regularly from Lutza's work.[255] Every Christmas Lou and Lutza gave the other a $1,000 check which they promptly endorsed over to the Fund.[256]

While the Smiths were sincere in their philanthropy, it also served a very pragmatic purpose. In 1949, for example, when virtually every religious group urged the General Court not to renew the track's gambling license, charitable organizations lined up to praise the Rock. Atty. J. Walker Wiggin, a director of the New Hampshire Society for Crippled Children and Handicapped Persons and former House Speaker of the General Court, told a legislative committee to renew the license.

"I am speaking definitely," Wiggin said, "on behalf of those crippled chil-

Gifts from the Smiths to the disabled children at the Kennedy Memorial Hospital.

dren who are now walking and tasting happiness because of the benefits from this aid." Over a twelve year period, Wiggin's group received $65,400 in donations from the track.[257]

In addition to war heroes, political bigwigs, and showbiz legends, there were lesser known, but equally colorful people associated with the Smiths and the Rock, like Mrs. Lou Palmer of Boston, known as Racetrack Lou and Mrs. William J. Foley, wife of the Boston district attorney. "I've won thousands and I've lost thousands," lamented Racetrack Lou, who often placed $100 bets. Overall, women contributed about 30 percent or $300,000, of the $1 million in bets placed in the first season.[258]

"The Lady in Red" also patronized the Rock. A woman always wearing "alluring" red dresses traveled the nation to watch the sport. She would start making bets at the $100 dollar window within five minutes of post time. At one track, the Lady in Red, reported an article in a Boston paper, purportedly told the clerk, "Just keep punching that damn thing till the bell rings and, believe me, mister, I hope they start late." Her bets totaled between $20,000 and $40,000.[259]

The "in" crowd dressed to be noticed.

The Rock may not have been Paris or New York, but it certainly had its own fashion etiquette. There could be, reported the *Boston Herald*, "flashy girls with long ear rings and giddy plaids who obviously are what they are . . . If you are going to a costume party some time soon the Rockingham racetrack is a good place to get ideas."[260] Another track observer remarked of the fashions that ladies could wear: "If the sun shines opening day, it'll be no brighter than the sunny lemon yellow stylists are touting this season. You'll see a lot of this gay hue—in blouses coordinated with printed or striped skirts—other appropriate colors—beiges, new tones of brown, soft and subtle blues and those always-smart black shoes—should have a medium heel."[261]

Gentlemen also followed a fashion code. "Mix-match outfits" were the rage in 1956, according to the same article, they included lightweight flannels and cottons for slacks. Sports jackets, of course, were a must for the fashionable gentleman of the day.[262]

A daily train from Boston brought thousands of patrons to the Rock. At departure time it was called the "post mortem" train.[263] Many came in hopes of overnight wealth. In 1959, however, a Haverhill, Massachusetts, man won

Mrs Smith, far right, with some of the community's social elite.

$23,336.20 on a $2 bet. It was the largest payoff on a $2 bet ever to occur in the United States.[264] The Rock was a place where dreams could come true.

Lou Smith, always sensitive to charges by the Rock's detractors, never stopped looking for public relations ideas to put the track in the most favorable light. In 1938, the track participated in the twentieth anniversary of the first air-mail flight. Young women at Rockingham Park sealed envelopes for the flight from the Rock to Lawrence, Massachusetts. The event proved quite popular among Granite Staters and newspapers throughout New Hampshire and other parts of New England covered the story.[265]

In the spring of the same year, *Rockingham*, a musical about the track presented by the Manchester Turn Verein, a local club, delighted audiences. A newspaper article reviewed the show: "The opening chorus included *Rockingham*, *Whistle While You Work*, and *Horses, Horses,* followed by the 'Jockey Girls.' The Jockey Girls, eight women, danced for the audience between numbers."[266] Writer Damon Runyon, for whom Walter Winchell later named the Cancer Fund, further helped to immortalize racetracks like the Rock. Runyon's fictional stories inspired one of the most popular Broadway musicals—*Guys and Dolls.*[267] Lou Smith is credited with starting the Damon Runyon Cancer Fund.[268]

Lou Smith atop a tower of aluminum pots and pans collected at the Rock on "Aluminum Day" in lieu of admission.

Smith even toyed with the idea of having an annual summer theater at his track. Crowds of more than 10,000, Smith predicted, would come to the Rock for Broadway-style musicals. He projected a weekly gross of $60,000. On the lawn, in front of the grandstand, Smith envisioned his track the summer home of Broadway celebrities. He contacted Broadway agent Lester Shurr. Archie Thompson, Shurr's colleague, explored the possibility and concluded the Rock had great

Lou Smith's contribution to a federal campaign to collect 20,000,000 pounds of aluminum to build tanks and planes for WWII bolstered his image and gained the Rock positive attention.

potential. Unfortunately, the dream never materialized. The schedule of harness and thoroughbred racing made it all but impossible to pull off a New Hampshire version of Broadway.[269] But Granite Staters loved reading about the possibility.

During World War II Smith identified another opportunity to win points with Granite Staters. The federal government initiated a campaign to collect 20,000,000 pounds of aluminum from the citizenry. The special collection supplemented normal aluminum supplies to build tanks and planes.[270] Smith embraced the campaign by requiring patrons to bring aluminum pots and pans on "Aluminum Day" as the cost of admission. The *Manchester Union* describe the concept:

> Aluminum is being collected for national defense. Lou Smith is anxious to do his small bit and sacrifice the entire gate receipts of opening day . . . Newspapers the country over are discussing the latest baby of the Smith brain with such great appreciation that "aluminum days" will certainly be staged in other parts of the country. The old Rock is the first institution on the continent devoted to sport that has contrived to tie its sports program in with the

One of Smith's many fundraising efforts to support the war.

defense of these shores, and he hereby donates the idea to the world, with no strings attached . . . News reels will be made of the historic event, for national distribution . . .[271]

In addition, the track purchased war bonds with any cash taken at the entry gate.

Throughout his life, Smith paid particular attention to veterans. "Every week we'd go down to Portsmouth and pick up a total of twenty wounded veterans from Pease and the Portsmouth Naval Hospital," reflected Mike Dagostino, and take them to the track. "Lou Smith would provide a bus and give each one $20. He'd wine and dine them." Dagostino remembered the same concern shown to veterans at the Chelsea Naval Hospital.[272]

"One day I was told by the captain in Boston," recalled Dagostino, "that some of the guys wanted radios and some didn't. I told that to Lou Smith. [Later] Mr. Smith called me into his office—'I just got 500 radios from Japan. They all have a little [ear plug] in them. Why don't you hand them out to the military?' So I handed out 250 radios to Portsmouth and 250 to the Chelsea Naval Hospital."[273]

Boston, Mass., October 16, 19 44   No. 32

THE FIRST NATIONAL BANK OF BOSTON 5-39
PAY TO THE ORDER OF

New Hampshire War Chest, Inc., Agent for
National War Fund, Inc. $ 100,445.61

NOT TO COVER 100,445 DOLLARS 61 CTS   Dollars

Smith used his considerable fundraising skills to benefit the war effort.

Lou Smith, center, receives an award from veterans.

Soldiers and the disabled were often given work at the Rock. "The money room," recalled Dagostino, "had disabled men—men who could sit and just count the money. They were in wheelchairs or used crutches."[274] World War I flying ace Col. C.E. Fauntleroy served as the track's treasurer.[275] Fauntleroy had been a pilot in the French Foreign Legion in the Sahara and later joined the U.S. Air Corps, where he trained Eddie Rickenbacker.[276]

Not surprisingly, Smith received numerous awards and certificates for his efforts on behalf of veterans. Due in large part to Smith's care for former soldiers, the track became a favorite stop for heroes such as Col. Gregory "Pappy" Boyington, a World War II ace and Medal of Honor winner. Boyington organized a top-notch squadron of aviators that helped to down twenty-eight Japanese planes in flight and another twenty-four on the ground.[277] Visits like this were always crowd pleasers.

Some of Lou Smith's antics brought smiles to thousands of fans. A few years before Smith died, he met with President Lyndon Johnson in Manchester. Smith handed the president a pair of his "snuggers," pieces of rubber cut from tubing to keep glasses from sliding down the nose. "You've already sent me six," Johnson told him, indicating that he was well aware of this New Hampshire legend. Smith had a habit of sending his invention to such celebri-

Fun-loving Smith tries his hand at playing the drums.

Comedian Jack E. Leonard with the Smiths.

Smith surveys the track in a quiet moment.

Smith was a devoted Red Sox fan.

ties as Pope Paul VI, Dwight Eisenhower, comedian Phil Silvers, TV personality Ed Sullivan, and talk show host Jack Paar.[278] Granite Staters could grin affectionately and think, "That's our Uncle Lou," as they read about him in the papers.

"Lou was everywhere," recalled Governor Gregg. He showed almost boundless energy at Rockingham Park as well. "He'd be at the windows. He'd be at the restaurant. He'd be down at the track."[279]

Smith further endeared himself in the hearts and minds of New Englanders with his devotion to the Red Sox. In 1949, the team was having a good year, and Smith informed the world, "The Rock will have to run itself for a little while. I'm neglecting my wife, my home, and my business because I have too many outside commitments. I'm helping McCarthy manage, Kinder pitch, Williams hit, and Zarilla field. In addition to all this, I'm turning some timely double plays and scheming how to get my hands on some World Series tickets . . . I'm a busy man. Much too busy to attend to my own affairs."[280] Granite Staters and track patrons relished these colorful stories. It was pure Lou Smith. It was New Hampshire.

It didn't matter if you were a politico, a racing fan, a celebrity watcher, a fashion fanatic. Everyone could find something of interest at the track. Rockingham Park created an unprecedented amount of color, glamour, and excitement. The Rock had it all.

CHAPTER 6

Lou and Lutza Smith

Everyone seemed to call the entrepreneurial, street-smart Lou Smith "my friend." Lou spent part of his boyhood in Paterson, New Jersey. According to many newspaper accounts, he was born in the United States. This is inaccurate. He emigrated with his family from Czarist Russia to either England or a British Commonwealth nation, perhaps Canada, before arriving in the United States. Naturalization papers indicate his citizenship as British and 1890 as his year of birth.[281] Louise Newman also recalled that Lou Smith had a twin sister born in Russia.[282] It appears that Lutza Smith, based on a photographic comparison, was about 15 years younger than her husband.

A photo of Lou and Lutza likely taken in the 1920s highlights Lutza's beauty and sense of fashion.

Smith described his father as "too religious and too lazy to be a good provider." This opinion, coupled with his falling out with a rabbi preparing him for bar mitzvah, encouraged him to leave his New Jersey home at a young age. He held various jobs before settling in Salem, New Hampshire: boxer, boxing promoter, dishwasher, circus hand, saloon keeper, motion picture distributor, whiskey salesman.[283] As a boxing promoter in Winnipeg, according to Damon Runyon, "Lou Smith hung up a record for an indoor gate that still stands in Canada, with Freddy Welsh, then lightweight champion of the world . . ."[284]

His entrepreneurial spirit and his love for the sport of racing materialized in his involvement with tracks throughout the country. He owned or retained an interest in tracks, at various stages of his life, in Vermont,[285] Las Vegas, New Jersey,[286] Texas, Massachusetts, and Canada.[287] Smith also served as general manager for a track in Havana, Cuba, in the late 1930s.[288]

Not all of Smith's financial endeavors were a success. Local political corruption made his Cuban track, Oriental Park, a hopeless business venture. The rise of Fidel Castro further complicated the management of the track.[289]

In contrast, Smith's Epsom Downs track in Texas proved a major success. Pugilist Jack Dempsey said that it had the "makings of one of the most beautiful plants in the country . . . [it] has the biggest future of any track in the [nation]."[290]

Epsom became "one of the biggest construction ventures completed in Houston in years,"[291] wrote a Texas newspaper. Gov. Miriam A. Ferguson and her husband, former governor Jim Ferguson,[292] joined approximately 30,000 people for opening day festivities. ". . . Cheering fans made a picture not soon to be forgotten,"wrote a reporter in the *Houston Post.* "The crowd overflowed the stand and club house and lined the fence enclosing the track for a distance of half a mile along the home stretch."[293]

Lloyd Gregory, sports editor for the *Houston Post,* described Lou Smith as "the outstanding racing promoter on the turf horizon today, and the state of Texas and the people of Houston are indeed lucky to have a man of his caliber as director of Houston's new Epsom Downs racetrack."[294]

Describing Smith's career, a Nevada newspaper wrote that, ultimately, religious forces in Texas succeeded in "eliminat[ing] horse racing in the state by balloting the sport out of existence" in 1938.[295] Political, not economic forces, ended the life of Epsom Downs.

The story was different in Nevada. Frank Wright, curator of manuscripts for the Nevada State Museum and Historical Society, noted that a palatial but bankrupt horse track in Las Vegas remained unfinished east of the Thunderbird Hotel. "What seemed to be the salvation of the project," he said, "came about because of a chance meeting in San Francisco between Lou Smith and

Lutza and Lou in a photo likely taken in Cuba in the 1930s when Lou served as general manager of a track in Havana.

Alfred Luke. Smith was the operator of famed Rockingham Park in New Hampshire, and Luke was prominent in California racing circles."[296]

Luke, a successful California attorney and thoroughbred enthusiast, and Smith raised $2 million. In 1953, construction resumed and Smith became president of the Las Vegas Jockey Club. "It was, for little Las Vegas," says Wright, "an extremely ambitious undertaking—comfortable seating for 20,000, a clubhouse, a swank restaurant, an escalator, and stables for a thousand horses. There were to be sixty-seven days of racing with very attractive purses."[297]

Despite some good racing with Willie Shoemaker and Anthony DeSpirito, though, attendance was poor. The first season competed with popular California tracks. On opening day, attendance was a mere 8,000 and by the following Monday it had dropped to 3,000. Soon unpaid contractors filed a series of lawsuits against the track which "led to the padlocking of the splendid track in October. Barley was planted on the track to keep it from blowing away. Whether the barley ever sprouted is unknown. What did sprout there was a convention center and a giant hotel,"[298] according to a Las Vegas paper.

Smith later commented on his Nevada venture: "I must have been some kind of a nut to think that a racetrack could operate next door to gambling halls."[299]

But despite the Las Vegas setback, Smith's reputation in the racing world never diminished. "Lou Smith is the creator of an industry or sport that became part of New Hampshire's character," said Alan Pope. Despite Lou Smith's

Smith receives an award from the New York Turf Writers in 1947.

involvement in tracks throughout North and South America, Rockingham Park remained his jewel and the one he owned until the end of his life. "There was nothing garish about Lou Smith," says Pope. "He was the right man to run the track and he was married to the right woman. Lou is a myth—not in a bad way—he's part of the New Hampshire scene, part of New Hampshire history."[300]

By the end of his career, Smith had earned awards for helping veterans and children for promoting understanding among Jews and Christians (Smith remained more of a cultural than a religious Jew his whole life), and for being one of the most influential promoters of horse racing. In 1948, he received the national title "Sportsman Who Did the Most for Racing" for his efforts to contain an outbreak of equine infectious anemia. In 1956, the Horsemen's Benevolent and Protection Association honored Smith as "one of its founding fathers"[301] Two years later jockey guilds throughout the nation named him "Man of the Year" for, among other things, making Rockingham Park the first track to offer insurance to riders.[302]

The New York Turf Writers honored him, as did their counterparts in New England. He received certificates of merit from the American Legion, Dis-

Dedication of the Lou and Lutza Smith Pavilion, October 1961.

abled American Veterans, Thoroughbred Racing Association, and the President's Committee on Employment of the Physically Handicapped (U.S. Department of Labor).[303]

In October 1961, His Eminence Cardinal Cushing of Boston dedicated the surgical unit at the Joseph P. Kennedy Memorial Hospital in Brighton, Massachusetts, in the name of Lou and Lutza Smith. The cardinal observed:

> In all my 40 years as a priest I have never met an individual like this good soul [Lou] until I met Lutza . . . one who was willing to assume all the work herself . . . writing letters day after day [regarding the annual clambake fund raisers for disabled children]; yes, sometimes all night. I don't know how she stands it. But I don't know what [we] would do without her here at the hospital.
>
> Not only does she give us money, but she sends us thousands of dollars worth of food every year. In other words, since she started this fund she has not only given us all of the money that she can collect but she has given us all of the gifts that she and Lou would have received for all of the various anniversaries, birthdays, wedding anniversaries, etc., that they would have

Lutza and Cardinal Cushing inside the pavilion.

had. Therefore, I want to be responsible for a memorial in their honor during their lifetime and my lifetime . . . I have never seen such dedicated, such
unselfish service.[304]

With such accolades, is it any wonder that Lou Smith never had a problem
renewing his gambling license?

Mike Dagostino also noted that "Cardinal Cushing told me that if it
weren't for Lou Smith, the Kennedy Memorial would be in trouble. He supported it eight months of the year."[305] The Kennedy clan gave the initial money
to start the hospital, but not the resources to keep it solvent.

Union Leader sportswriter Bob Hilliard wrote in 1967, "In his own unob-
trusive way, Lou Smith has probably done more for the State of New Hampshire than any other man alive. He has brought us wealth, he has helped our
poor, our orphaned children, our education."[306]

Louise Newman, Smith's secretary, reflected that Lou Smith was "wonderful to work for—easygoing. He had a beautiful office, which he never used. He
used to sit right next to my desk, read the newspapers, and drink his coffee. He

was very casual. He had no outside interests. His whole life was business."[307]

Despite the informality, Louise Newman recalled a certain reverence for him: "A lot of people called him Uncle Lou, but the employees called him Mr. Smith. I called him Mr. Smith."[308]

Lou and Lutza lived in a rather modest, but comfortable, apartment at the racetrack. The apartment was located on the top floor in the same building where most of the administrative offices are still housed today. An outside porch or walkway overlooking the field connected the apartment to Lou Smith's office. Although unused today, the apartment suggests that despite the power and wealth Smith acquired during his life, he remained a simple man. For a time the Smiths also kept apartments in Florida and New York City.

"Mr. Smith was good to people," recalled Rockingham County Commissioner Ernie Barka. "I know people he loaned money to. The guy was good to the town. I admired Lou Smith."[309] Sen. Stewart Lamprey noted that "people still speak of Lou Smith like a saint. He had a heart of gold."[310]

In April 1969, Lou Smith died. Atty. Kenneth F. Graf became president of the New Hampshire Jockey Club; Richard M. O'Dowd, general manager of Rockingham Park.[311]

Gov. and Mrs. Walter Peterson and former governors John W. King and Hugh Gregg led the New Hampshire delegation to the service at Temple Emanuel in Lawrence, Massachusetts.[312] To the very end of his life, Smith remained actively involved in horse racing. At the time of his death he served as president and chairman of the board of the New Hampshire Jockey Club Inc., vice president and general manager of the New Hampshire Trotting and Breeding Association Inc., chairman of the board for the Taconic Trotting and Breeding Association Inc., and the operator of Green Mountain Park in Pownal, Vermont.[313]

More than 1,000 people[314] attended the services, including nuns, jockeys, New England track officials, former Red Sox player Duffy Lewis, and Suffolk County District Attorney Garrett Byrnes.[315] Two nephews served as bearers, along with Atty. Kenneth F. Graf , N.F. Bigelow Jr., Robert G. Little, William Freeman, Patrick Giordans, and Atty. Maurice Simon.[316]

New Hampshire House Minority Leader Robert Raiche observed, "Rockingham is one of the few tracks where you can take your wife. It's decent, clean and well run, equal to a ski area."[317] Emmett J. Kelley, New Hampshire Racing Commission chair, reflected, "I cast the first vote in the State Senate for racing when the bill was first introduced. Lou's contribution to the economy of the state and the industry he brought to the state is of tremendous value. Together with his many philanthropies, his presence was felt in every community. "[318]

Governor Gregg observed, "When you look at Lou you say, 'Yeah, this is big time gambling,' but as you get to know him you realize, here's a guy who is

*A family portrait that is believed to be Lutza (center in dark dress) embraced by
her mother.*

as honest and clean as anybody could ever possibly be—decent and human,
very compassionate, a man of good judgment."[319]

"He had a reputation for personal honesty," recalled Governor Peterson.
"He had good standards and a sense of responsibility to the community. You
hear all kind of things when a person dies. But you never heard any of that
stuff when Lou Smith died. He was about as good a person as you could
have."[320]

"Mrs. Smith," recalled Louise Newman, "went into almost permanent
mourning. She lived alone in the apartment. She fell one night and broke her
hip. After the hospital she went to a nursing home in Lawrence and later to
Salem. Mrs. Smith never went back to the track."[321]

Mrs. Newman described Lutza Smith as a "sharp lady." But Mrs. Smith
also appeared to be, even before Lou's death, a lonely woman. Despite her work
on behalf of disabled children, she had few friends. "Lutza was a lady with a lot
of grace," recalled Alan Pope. "She did a lot for charity. It came from her
heart."[322]

"I married the Rock of Gibraltar," Lou Smith told Mike Dagostino.

Lutza Smith walking with one of her "angels."

Dagostino reflected, "She lived for the cardinal and his children. She talked about it 365 days a year." Mrs. Smith "only had one thing in life—to take care of those kids," he said.[323] Lutza Smith, described by some who knew and interacted with her as difficult and introverted, died in 1984.

Lou and Lutza gave Rockingham Park its personality. They gave it a cer-

Lou and Lutza with Cardinal Cushing at the Kennedy Hospital in Boston.

tain romance. Both remained highly public figures, loved by all, but still private and enigmatic. Everyone at the State House knew Lou Smith, the great entrepreneur who exemplified rugged individualism. To many Granite Staters, Lou, with the soul of a Yankee, and his wife, Lutza, with a heart of gold, were household names. But this was only part of the aura that the Smiths created. There was also the sport itself.

CHAPTER 7

Sport of Royalty

"There's a certain romance to horse racing," says Edward Callahan, current general manager for Rockingham Park. "Look at the Saratoga meet. They have [tens of thousands of] people in August and it's not because they're all gamblers. The romance of the horse is part of it."[324] Rockingham Park, from its beginning meet in 1933, provided an allure with some of the finest thoroughbred racing in the nation.

"Smashing three track records in a complete reversal of form," wrote a sportswriter at the Rock, "long shots thundered home in six of the seven races on

Wetting down the track before the crowds arrive.

the program to delight a crowd of about 5,000 which paid no attention to sweltering heat here this afternoon."[325] In the fall of 1933, "thoroughbreds valued at more than $2,000,000" were at the track,[326] according to an article in the *Boston Post*. During the meet, purses reached $156,000 with a daily average of $5,000.[327] More than 385,000 fans attended races at the Rock during the 1933 season.[328]

The *Boston Globe* reported of the fall 1933 meet: "Many of the country's leading colts and fillies will be making their New England debut at this meeting . . . In fact, the caliber of the horses at this meeting is so outstanding that some of the stars in the early summer meeting will be taking back seats now that Sheldon Fairbank's Gold Step, Cornelius V. Whitney's Halcyon, Frederic Burton's Wiser Daughter and many other crack performers are groomed for the big stakes."[329]

Numerous sportswriters expressed this enthusiasm in articles throughout Lou Smith's involvement with the track. As another example, the *Boston Herald* reported of one fall race: "Only 15 years old and looking even five years less than that, baby-faced Jackie Westrope, the nation's most sensational jockey, staged a brilliant demonstration of riding as Rockingham's 25-day thoroughbred horse-race meeting opened this afternoon before a crowd of 12,000."[330]

Four records were shattered on inaugural day, the first being the Speed Handicap. "Glorify, a three-year old filly, from the Middlebury stables . . . galloped the five furlong distance in 1:00 4-5."[331] Once again, Lou Smith attracted national attention for New Hampshire.

The newspapers touted the entrants with superlatives. Seabiscuit, "king of the handicap horses," ran at Rockingham Park.[332] Teufel, "one of the top handicap stars in the country," High Velocity, Sweeping Light, Roman Soldier,[333] Man O' War, and War Admiral[334] also delighted racing enthusiasts. And what racing fan could forget Brass Monkey, who "specialized in coming as much as 20 lengths [from behind] to win."[335]

Famous jockeys appearing at the Salem track included Charles Maffeo, Leroy Moyers, Mike Carrozzella, Henry Wajda, Fernando Fernandez, Bob Ussery, and Bill Shoemaker, the latter being the "winningest jockey in history."[336] Eddie Arcaro, five time winner of the Kentucky Derby, and Sammy Boulmetis, who earned more than $12 million in purse money,[337] raced at Rockingham Park. Tony DeSpirito, who set a world record by bringing home 390 winners in 1952, learned to ride at the Rock and became one of the favorite jockeys at the track. Their names were magic in the racing world and virtually guaranteed throngs of patrons.[338]

The Rock became a favorite stomping ground for Mrs. Payne Whitney, owner of the renowned Greentree stable. The Whitney family were the leading breeders in North America. Col. E.R. Bradley of Kentucky, described by a Manchester newspaper as owner of "more Kentucky Derby winners than any

Sports writers in the press room at the Rock.

other man in history" also brought his thoroughbreds to Rockingham Park in 1938.[339] Movie mogul Louis B. Mayer sent thirty of his finest thoroughbreds to the Rock in 1939.[340]

Dave Wilson, of the *Boston Advertiser*, wrote, "Great horses, great riders, a great racing secretary, a strong stewards' stand, a fine starter . . . the public can be pardoned for expecting the finest in horse-racing. And back of it all, responsible for it all, is the pioneer, Lou Smith."[341]

Eventually, other New England tracks looked to Lou Smith, perhaps a bit jealously, as an innovator. He brought such devices as turnstiles, totalizators, and starting gates to the sport. He also streamlined racing by eliminating post parades because they wasted time.[342] Closed circuit televisions became a standard at racetracks throughout the country due, in part, to Smith's introduction of the technology for both thoroughbred and harness racing.

There was also the "tire patrol" at the Rock: teams of employees who would look for flat tires on the cars of patrons in the gigantic parking lot and repair them at no charge.[343] Smith also provided complimentary transportation from the parking lot to the track.[344]

(photo left) Willie Shoemaker, chats with an adoring fan at the Rock. (photo right)
In 1952 19-year-old Ronnie Ferraro makes his New England debut in the New
England Futurity at Rockingham Park.

Smith kept parents who arrived with youngsters happy with Rocking Horse
Park, a childcare center staffed by qualified personnel who fed and entertained
children while Mom and Dad watched the races.[345] Two trained and registered
nursery attendants helped youngsters ride Francis the Mule who had served as
a Hollywood stand-in for famed animal star Francis, in several Donald O'Con-
nor movies.[346]

A Rhode Island newspaper credited Smith with introducing the "2 year
old racing card" in 1955. It was another first in the racing world. "I hope," said
Smith, "to make Rockingham the leader in racing for younger thoroughbreds."[347] He marketed the Rock as the ideal place for young horses. "I'm going
the derby distance with this idea," the sportsman noted. "I want the future
champions to run at the Rock . . . Our air, our climate, our water, and our
clover are unsurpassed and they will serve as a tonic for young thoroughbreds."[348]

In 1967, approximately one million people visited the Rock, making it the
top tourist attraction in the Granite State. During that season, two years before
Lou Smith's death, the top three-year-olds in the country raced at Rockingham
Park—"more than entered the triple crown events—the Kentucky Derby, the
Preakness, and the Belmont,"[349] wrote the *Union Leader*. Fourteen hundred
thoroughbreds participated in the Rock's thirty-fifth season that year.[350]

The Rock's 1967 season is significant for another reason. The Red Sox had
made it to the World Series. Not an empty seat could be found at Fenway that
year. One sportswriter, keeping in mind that the Rock had become the top
tourist attraction in New Hampshire and one of the largest in New England,

*Famous trainer
Max Hirsch with
Lou Smith.*

wrote: "The fantastic chase to the top by the colorful Red Sox still didn't blunt a record season at Rockingham . . . If there were ever any doubts about the appeal of Rockingham (or of harness racing), they have been dispelled by this dramatic showdown . . . Even the Red Sox in their greatest moments could not stem the tide to Rockingham."[351]

Although the Red Sox went on to lose the World Series 4 to 3 to St. Louis,[352] the Rock never let down the fans. The average nightly attendance just for harness racing exceeded 8,000. Three attendance records were broken in 1967.[353]

. Smith's promotion of harness racing attracted attention throughout the nation and the world. He brought harness champions from as far as New Zealand.[354] Two of Canada's top standardbreds, Tie Silk and Champ Volvo, wowed crowds in 1961.[355] In the same year, William "Buddy" Gilmore of Hamburg, New York, the 1959 "national champion" standardbreds and Marcel Dostie, one of Canada's leading harness drivers, also dazzled crowds at the Rock.[356] Johnny Chapman, Jimmy Cruise, and Alfred "Bucky" Day were other star harness drivers.[357]

"Records of all sorts tumbled here at Rockingham Park last night [at the harness meet]," wrote one sports reporter in April 1960. "A record attendance of 13,791 saw traffic to traffic moving bumper to bumper from all points of the compass."[358]

During the April 1960 season, a Massachusetts newspapers hailed one of the horses: Tidemite "became one of the nation's leading pacers breaking all track records as the 5 yr. old paced the mile in 2:02.3 to not only break the track record but to also turn in the fastest mile of the year on any track."[359]

In 1961, at the Isles of Shoals Handicap, Bay Goose and Poker Chip, "the sensational pacers from the strong stable of C.D. Higgins of South Windsor, Conn" were the star horses, a reporter wrote in the *Morning Union Leader*.[360] In 1967, more superlatives: "a classy field of trotters [went] to the post in the $6,000 Invitational Newport Trot at Rockingham Park tonight. The entries include the unbeaten Canadian ace Danny Song . . ."[361] And there was also Scottish Design, voted California Pacer of the year in 1966,[362] Maynard the Miller, Skipper Gene, and Great Credit, racing in 1967.[363]

Roberta "Bobbe" Huntress, harness driver and former schoolteacher from Gouverneur, New York, showed some moxie that endeared her to Rock patrons. Because of her gender, Massachusetts denied her a racing license. With typical New York gusto and bravura, she ignored her detractors and raced in the Live Free or Die state.[364]

On one occasion a sportswriter at the Rock recalled that when harness drivers were registering in the racing secretary's office, the clerk looked up and remarked, "'We're only taking the names of drivers, lady,' as a diminutive young woman stepped up to sign the form. The young lady brushed aside the remark and stepped right up and signed the form, Bobbe Huntress."[365] In addition to her chutzpa, Granite Staters came to know her for winning four open handicaps with Wee Irish. The horse earned $11,970, "an all-time record for money earned by a trotter at any one Rockingham meeting," according to a newspaper article.[366]

Lou Smith seemed to have a constant concern for the quality of horses at his track. As early as 1949, he banned all thoroughbreds three years and older that had raced at least eight times within a two-year period but didn't finish third at least one time. Rockingham Park became the first track in the nation with a rule that banned "galloping glue-pots," as they were colorfully termed in the *Dover Democrat*.[367]

In 1955, Smith introduced the New England Futurity—a special race only for thoroughbred horses raised in the region.[368] And in 1963 he introduced a classification system for harness racing that replaced a letter classification. It was used for the first time in New England. Three categories described entries—claiming races, condition races, and open races. "Claiming" referred to the value of the horse as determined by the owner or his agent. "Condition" referred to the gait (trotter or pacer), age, sex, money winnings, and number of races won. And the "open" category classified the fastest horses at the meet.[369]

Rockingham Park..May 9, 1960..Trot..One Mile: 2.05.4

Smith hands driver Andy Foster a trophy after Sumter Prince trotted to victory with a 2.05.4 mile.

Because of Smith's innovations, marketing creativity, and willingness to make almost any accommodation for horse breeders and owners, stall space for harness and thoroughbred meets was always scarce. It wasn't unusual for stall space demand to exceed availability, "which makes for better racing," wrote a reporter, "as the less capable horses can be weeded out."[370]

Smith didn't just put Salem on the map: he also made a permanent contribution to the sport. The Horsemen's Benevolent and Protective Association traces its founding to Rockingham Park. In 1940, Smith spearheaded the Horse Retirement Fund. It later became an organization with more than 17,000 members consisting of owners, trainers, and breeders in Canada and the United States. The mission was to purchase aged horses to live out the rest of their lives grazing. Smith donated 1 percent of every winning purse to buy horses for retirement.[371]

He even received accolades for how he treated jockeys and harness drivers. Although his was the oldest New England track, Smith had housing and accommodations for these riders that were second to none. "Lou Smith once again remembers 'the forgotten men of racing' and gives them living conditions that are unequaled anywhere in the United States,"[372] wrote one observer, referring to the provisions made for jockeys.

"Mr. Racing"

"MR. FUTURITY"

It is entirely fitting and proper that the man who brought pari-mutuel racing to the New England scene, should also be the father of its sportiest race — the New England Futurity.

When Lou Smith announced ten years ago his plan for a New England race for home-foaled two-year-olds there were those who argued that the breeding industry in the area could never supply enough racing talent to perpetuate the event. But for Smith, it presented a stimulus to the breeding industry, a challenge to be met by New England breeders.

Today's talented list of nominations more than justifies Lou Smith's faith in these dedicated men and women who have done so much to improve the standard of the sport in the area.

From a modest start with a $5,000 purse ten years ago, the Futurity of 1961 has become an important event on the turf calendar with a $25,000-added price tag.

Smith's popular persona was linked with the Rock and the events held there.

The men and women involved in horses and racetracks observed Edward Callahan, today's general manager and vice president for Rockingham Park, "care more for their animals than anything else. The people right next to them [in neighboring stalls] are always willing to help. These people care for one another. They'll do anything they possibly can for each other and for their animals. Whether they have money or time, these people are sincere. They care. And they work very hard."373

"It takes a lot of effort to show up at 4:30 in the morning and get your horses fed, get them ready to train, and maybe not get out of here until 12 or 1 in the morning," Callahan added. "You need a quality horse, but at the same time, if you don't treat the horse right, he won't win. These people are fighting to make a life for themselves. And they do it very honestly." It's part of the romance of racing that the patrons may not see or fully appreciate.374 But Lou Smith never forgot the challenges many faced to make ends meet.

In 1956, Smith opened a new clubhouse—one of many renovations during his tenure as the Rock's general manager. It "glistens in glass and aluminum and sheer beauty," wrote one sports reporter. "It will spoil the hardy, old race-goer by introducing him to a lifetime of soft, sweet luxury at no advance in the cost of admittance."375

Unlike many other clubhouses throughout the nation, the Rock's 1956 structure lacked poles to block anyone's view. The staircase, the only one of its kind in the nation, cost $75,000. Builders used only the finest Italian marble. When completed, 12,000 square feet of glass, 4,800 cubic yards of concrete, 250 tons of structural steel, and 155 tons of reinforcing rods had been used.376 Ever conscious of the public's perception, Smith instituted a policy not to hire anyone over 75 years of age to work at his glistening new clubhouse. Instead, "the new clubhouse will be staffed with natty youngsters who will fit better into the atmosphere,"377 he declared.

"I hope," wired Red Sox star Joe Cronin to Lou Smith after being inducted into the Baseball Hall of Fame in Cooperstown, New York, "that your million dollar clubhouse will be a Hall of Fame for you."378 "The new clubhouse," wrote the *Lawrence Eagle Tribune*, "makes obsolete every other clubhouse from here to Florida."379

Lou Smith's "new club house," wrote the *Boston Record*, "has created a sensation in turf circles and is expected to result in vast new building programs at tracks throughout the entire country . . . It is the last word in both beauty and comfort . . ."380 Even in faraway New York, folks took note. "The comforts and convenience," wrote Jack McGrath of the *Troy Times Record*, [are exceptional], "it offers the answers to a racetrack follower's most fervent dreams . . . it is the last word in modern construction . . . The accomplishments are of giant proportions and worthy of the highest praise."381

According to Louise Newman, secretary to Lou Smith, "Rockingham Park was smaller than Saratoga Springs, but probably prettier. It was a gorgeous track. A thing of beauty."[382] Alan Pope, chief of staff to two governors, noted that "Rockingham had a personality like Churchill Downs—'My Old Kentucky Home.' The track stood as sort of a symbol—the soul of New Hampshire."[383]

The Rock had earned the respect of breeders and racing enthusiasts throughout North America. Although it did not possess the history of tracks in Kentucky and Saratoga Springs, the innovations, both administrative and technological pioneered at Rockingham Park, coupled with the quality of the horses, did indeed make it an unquestioned leader in the racing world. Atty. Robert Shaines, of Portsmouth, noted, "Lou Smith developed Rockingham into a major, national racing facility. It was certainly known throughout the racing industry as one of the better tracks in the country."[384]

CHAPTER 8

Rock's Decline and Future

In 1969, the year of Lou Smith's death, Bill Veeck, president of nearby Suffolk Downs outside Boston, started the great track war. Throughout Lou Smith's life, Rockingham Park, Suffolk Downs, and two Rhode Island tracks had avoided an all out war with one another by staggering the scheduling of meets. But under Veeck, Suffolk Downs's racing schedule competed directly with the Rock. Other tracks were forced to expand their racing seasons to stay competitive.[385]

Revenues increased at the tracks, but the average daily handle dropped. According to one Rhode Island paper, "It is evident that the drop in the daily handle is a result of a corresponding drop in attendance." The top thoroughbreds no longer raced at New England tracks.[386]

Threats of track wars date back to 1938.[387] But it seems that Lou Smith played an important role in keeping all of them content or at least other track owners were too timid to take him on. He ensured that New Hampshire had a large, dependable source of revenue.[388] In 1959, for example, Smith negotiated a truce. According to one New Hampshire paper, ". . . those in the know say that a very uneasy truce is existing among the four major racetracks in the New England circuit . . ."[389]

In 1955, B.A. Dario, president and treasurer of Lincoln Downs, purportedly delivered an ultimatum to officials both at Suffolk Downs and at Rockingham Park. Neither track cared.[390] Seven years later, Dario complained loudly, "Year in and year out Suffolk and Rockingham get the lush, warm weather dates, and Rhode Island tracks get the cold leftovers." The Rock had a July to September season for its thoroughbreds and March to May and mid-September to late October for its harness meets.[391]

A few weeks before Dario publicly complained, Smith said, "This threatened racing war will not bother us here in New Hampshire. We will have some real surprises for those people in Rhode Island,"[392] he added snickering.

An article in a Sunday New Hampshire paper said, "If Lou Smith and his associates usually seem to come out of the annual New England 'date war' in solid shape, with prime racing dates, it could be because Rockingham is 'lead-

The remnants of the Rock's clubhouse after the 1980 fire.

ing from strength.' That strength is the tremendous backlog of public good will, the good 'corporate image' which Madison Avenue strives to achieve. It is certainly no accident in a 'dog eat dog' business."[393]

Smith always had the upper hand. His negotiating skills, ongoing innovations at the Rock, his eye on keeping patrons comfortable, and always making sure he had the best available horses at his track gave him little to worry about.

"Lou Smith was the king of the racing industry," Mike Dagostino said. "He designated the days. Whatever Uncle Lou said went."[394]

Salvatore A. Rizzo, owner of Berkshire Downs in Hancock, Massachusetts, charged that Lou Smith didn't conduct business fairly. He contended that Smith's track in nearby Pownal, Vermont, would ruin his business: "Smith is presently dedicated to the destruction of Hancock in order that Pownal can survive . . . Mr. Smith will sit back and laugh as Massachusetts residents stream across the border into Vermont. And when he tires of chuckling there, he will move back to Rockingham where his hilarity will be equally as loud while Massachusetts fills up the New Hampshire state coffers.[395]

In reality, however, Lou Smith never engaged in unscrupulous business

Rockingham Park today. Opening day June 11, 1995.

practices. But he knew better than anyone else how to stay competitive and run the best horse track in New England.

Eventually, competition from tracks in other states did take its toll. By the early 1970s, an informal agreement on non-overlapping racing meets, which had always limited the competition among tracks through scheduling racing seasons that did not overlap, ended. Massachusetts and Rhode Island expanded to two hundred days of racing. Ray Poirier, Rockingham's public relations director, lamented, "Because of these conflicts the racetrack operation feels the economic squeeze."396

In the spring of 1973, Atty. William Phinney, board member and legal counsel for Rockingham Park, asked for help from the state by increasing the track's share of the betting handle. He said, "We're the highest taxpayer in New Hampshire . . . there's no secret about that." In the prior year the state received almost $9 million from pari-mutuel betting taxes from the Rock. On a $2 bet, $1.68 went to the winning bettor. The state received 16 cents, the owners of the track and the horsemen each 8 cents.397

William Loeb, of the *Union Leader*, blasted the idea as the work of "a heavily financed lobbying operation . . . at the track and in the Legislature to alter [an] equitable arrangement."[398] The track had lost much of its clout. It no longer supplied a major portion of the budget with tax revenue. The impact of Gov. Peterson's Business Profits Tax (BPT) passed in the early 1970s now had a major impact on state finances.

On July 29, 1980, eleven years after Lou Smith's death, a disastrous fire destroyed much of the Rock. Projections placed the yearly tax revenue loss at $5 million for the state and Salem's loss at $480,000 or about 3 percent of its tax base.[399] The town lost another $40,000 in licensing fees.[400] Salem town manager Donald Jutton lamented about the psychological impact saying, "Rockingham is so intricately interwoven with the identity of Salem."[401]

One New Hampshire newspaper commented caustically: "Our first and admittedly antisocial and unfair reaction when we first heard of the fire at Rockingham Park racetrack was that the state of New Hampshire may be forced into making an honest living."[402]

George Gillman, commissioner of the state Resources and Economic Development Department, reflected, "Rockingham was a reason for so many people coming to the state. It's been a landmark."[403] The state had been receiving about $90,000 a day during the racing season from a track that once employed, on average, five hundred people and provided 1,500 horsemen a place to race.[404]

The Rock remained closed for almost four years until Rockingham Venture Inc. purchased the track in August 1983 and built new facilities. Racing resumed at the Rock on May 26, 1984,[405] and continues to this day. But Rockingham has lost its mystique, along with the larger-than-life personalities once associated with it. Casinos, video gambling, and off-track betting, as well as competition from other tracks, have limited its competitiveness. Today, New England's oldest racetrack, like so many others around the nation, struggles to stay in the black.[406]

Ed Callahan, general manager for the Rock, contends that there remains "a tremendous amount of potential. The state could have the good old days of racing again if they recognized that potential. The introduction of other forms of gaming here would make for one of the top facilities in the country. If they don't recognize it, then it will be very difficult for racing to maintain itself."[407]

CHAPTER 9

What a Finish!

Lou Smith's Rockingham Park made an enormous contribution to the economic vitality of New Hampshire, and its history still offers many timeless lessons about society, government, and human nature.

Revenue concerns are as much a part of the state budget process now as they were more than sixty years ago. Other issues Granite Staters grappled with decades ago are also being revisited. In 1996, as noted earlier, several New Hampshire gubernatorial candidates, for example, debated whether video gambling should be introduced; others discussed the role of government and downsizing it to save money; some expressed concerns about the influence of organized crime on legal gambling. History has come full circle. The 1997 New Hampshire Supreme Court's decision that finds the reliance on property taxes unconstitutional as a means to pay for education further complicates the process of raising revenue in a state that has neither an income or a sales tax.

Sportswriter Damon Runyon, of the *New York Press*, wrote, "Lou Smith is one of the best liked men in any field of sport . . . As the Master of Rockingham Park he will give the people of New Hampshire something to brag about."[408] For more than thirty-five years Lou and Lutza Smith provided Granite Staters glamour, excitement, and escape from the realities of life. And perhaps just as importantly, Lou Smith created jobs at his track, encouraged commercial development in a small community, and pumped more than $100 million into the state treasury. The track played a critical role in staving off the imposition of a broadbased tax. The Rock was indeed something for Granite Staters to brag about.

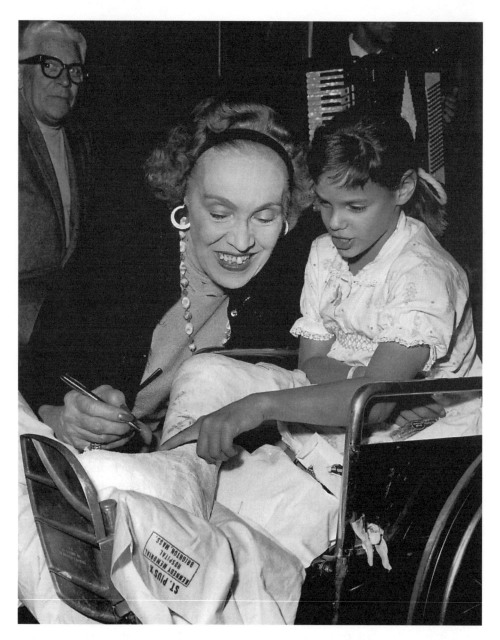

Lutza signs the cast of a patient at Kennedy Memorial Hospital.

Beyond Rockingham, The Smith Legacy

THE LOU AND LUTZA SMITH CHARITABLE FOUNDATION

During their lifetimes, Lou and Lutza Smith gave generously to a broad spectrum of charitable causes but their focus was on helping needy children—"God's sick angels," as Lutza lovingly referred to them. It was perhaps Lou and Lutza Smith's greatest sorrow that they did not have children of their own, but that sadness and the outlet that they found for it translated into an enormous benefit for many thousands of disadvantaged and disabled children throughout New Hampshire and Massachusetts.

According to George Carney, a personal adviser to Lou in the heady days of the 1960s, Lutza was "completely dedicated to helping children." She was "always on the go, running off to visit children in hospitals." And, he adds, "she didn't hesitate to ask some of the wealthier people [with whom] she came in contact to make donations to various causes." It seems they never said no to Lutza.

Helping needy and disabled children was, indeed, the driving force of her life. "She was like Mother Teresa," Carney says, an interesting image for the "finest dressed woman on the turf," as she was sometimes described, often dripping with glitz and glamour. Lutza was, to many, the embodiment of contradiction: Mother Teresa in jewels; a private woman living in a very public arena; a stylish clotheshorse who otherwise lived modestly; a "sharp lady" with a soft heart.

Lou's motivation for giving was, clearly, more complicated than was Lutza's, but he lacked none of his wife's sincerity. Prior to his death, Lou established the framework for the Lou and Lutza Smith Charitable Foundation. It wasn't until Lutza's death in 1984 that the Foundation was fully funded with upwards of $4 million in assets. There was one interesting and unique provision written into the terms and conditions of the Trust: The entire sum, interest and principal, was to be fully expended within fifteen years of the date of Lutza's death. The task of disbursing the money fell to the Foundation trustees.

It was not the Smiths' style in life, nor apparently, in death, to do things on anything but a grand scale. No trusts in perpetuity; they wanted the money spent and the impact of their gift to be felt. And it has been.

*Thoroughbred Watch It Grow was registered under the colors of Lutza Smith's
Crippled Children's Non-Sectarian Fund. All purse money won by the horse
went into the fund, while trainer Sid Bernstein (left) absorbed the expense of
racing the animal.*

The original trustees of the Lou and Lutza Smith Charitable Foundation
were Kenneth Graf, senior partner in the New Hampshire law firm of
McLane, Graf, Raulerson & Middleton, legal counsel to the Smiths, and suc-
cessor to the position of general manager, Rockingham; Arthur Green, who
served for only a brief period before succumbing to illness; Charles DeGrandpre, senior partner in the law firm of McLane, Graf; and, in lieu of Mr. Green's
serving, the Very Reverend Edward J. Carney.

Current/successor trustees include Charles DeGrandpre; Louise Newman,
secretary to Mr. Smith; and attorney Kathleen Robinson of Portsmouth, N.H.

It was, at the time of the Foundation's establishment, Ken Graf's opinion
that the fifteen year timetable would, by necessity, have to be accelerated. Given
the overwhelming responsibility and time requirements needed to review grant
applications and make evaluations for the appropriate dissemination of funds,
he believed it best for the trustees to concentrate their efforts within a shorter
time frame. The period recommended: two to three years.

It was with this concern that the trustees made their key decision. By unanimous vote the board determined to contract with the New Hampshire Charitable Foundation (NHCF) in Concord for all administrative/staff support functions. According to Charles DeGrandpre it was, "one of the best decisions we could have made."

Present for the first trustee meeting, held August 5, 1985, were: Graf, DeGrandpre, Reverend Carney, and Louise Newman, as well as two staff members from the New Hampshire Charitable Foundation. As reflected in the minutes from this meeting, trustees determined that all inquiries and applications to the Smith Foundation would be received and acknowledged by the NHCF. NHCF staff also took over responsibility for the solicitation of all additional information from grant applicants as might be needed for further review by trustees.

Additionally, all applicants presented to the trustees would include evaluative comments and recommended action prepared by senior officers of NHCF. Last, Charitable Foundation staff would forward grant payments, ensure that grant purposes were met, and obtain completion reports on funded projects.

With the support of NHCF, the trustees were freed from all administrative functions while remaining in full control of the assets of the Foundation. The ultimate decision-making power with regard to project funding rested with the trustees alone.

Although the Smith Foundation had been designated a General Purpose Fund, the New Hampshire Charitable Foundation set forth specific parameters for application guidelines. "Without some sort of narrowing focus," Attorney DeGrandpre notes, "we would have been all over the map." His words have literal as well as figurative connotations. The guidelines were established in an effort to maintain continuity with interests and the work accomplished by the Smiths during their lifetimes. They stated that priority would be given to organizations located in and serving the State of New Hampshire and to those active in areas that had interested the Smiths. Funding consideration was given to programs and projects that:

- Enhanced social and educational services for children with special needs resulting from mental, physical, or emotional disabilities and for their families;
- Aided in the prevention of child abuse and neglect;
- Improved health care for children who did not receive adequate services because of poverty or other barriers;
- Worked in areas of advocacy, public education, and reform directed at creating more effective child-serving institutions and systems statewide;
- Were related to the conduct and operation of horse racing.

The Smith Foundation money was fully expended in 1996, twelve years from the date of establishment. In all, grants totaling more than $5.6 million (the Foundation funds were invested conservatively, with accrued interest totaling approximately $1.6 million) were made to more than 270 organizations. The list of those who have benefited is impressive and certainly in keeping with what had been the Smiths' focus. The couple's "larger than life" personae can be seen to this day in the impact that their Foundation has made; an impact that can be measured child by child, person by person.

As stated in the minutes from the August 15, 1985, meeting, William Hart Jr. then of the NHCF, is recognized as saying foundation grants to charitable organizations in amounts from $10,000 to $50,000 are rare in New Hampshire. He goes on to say that it is his belief that providing support at that level would be a particularly useful role for the Smith Foundation. And, indeed, it has been.

Two of the last and largest grants awarded by the Smith Foundation were made in 1996 to the New Hampshire Children's Trust and the Harry Alan Gregg Foundation at Crotched Mountain.

The grant to the New Hampshire Children's Trust was in the amount of $500,000. At the time of its granting, Charles DeGrandpre is quoted as saying, "This is the largest award the Smith Foundation has made in its history. The grant will strengthen community programs for family support and child abuse prevention throughout New Hampshire."

Not only did the grant strengthen existing community programs, but, according to Lisa Brenna, executive director of the Children's Trust, it also "dramatically increased the number of non-profit organizations that the Trust has been able to fund." In 1995, the New Hampshire Children's Trust granted $55,000 to aid child-related nonprofit agencies. Following the 1996 receipt of the Smith Foundation grant, the amount expended rose to $90,000. But it was not until 1997 that the impact of the Smith award was fully realized. Funds granted by the Children's Trust in 1997 alone exceeded $181,000.

The award to the Harry Alan Gregg Foundation at Crotched Mountain was in the amount of $400,000. Following its receipt, Gregg Foundation funds available to provide direct financial assistance to individuals with handicaps nearly doubled. A letter of thanks, written by the parents of a Gregg Foundation grant recipient states, in part:

> [In] January 1997, you approved a grant for our son to purchase a Vocal Assistant. [T]his device has vastly improved [his] communication . . . He seems to really enjoy having the power of speech [and] is getting very good at expressing his wants and needs . . . He is now able to ask to go to McDonalds, tell us he needs to use the rest room or that he needs help with something. He has even learned to turn the volume up when he doesn't get a response . . . We would like to thank [you] very much for helping us open this door for our son.

A brief listing of other organizations that have benefited from the Smiths' charity include: Child Health Services, Concord Area Trust for Community Housing, Portsmouth Prenatal Clinic, Families First Program, New Hampshire Healthy Kids Corp, Child and Family Services of New Hampshire, Big Brothers/Big Sisters, Durham Infant Center, Children's Shelter, Task Force Against Domestic and Sexual Violence, Children's Alliance of New Hampshire, Concord Community Arts School, David's House at Dartmouth-Hitchcock Medical Center, University of New Hampshire Equine Center, The Eighth Pole (to support substance abuse and primary health care programs for workers at Rockingham Park), and The Racetrack Ministry (for support of the Child Care Center for employees of Rockingham Park).

Few have done more than Lou and Lutza Smith in changing for the better the lives of New Hampshire's disadvantaged children. They did not know all, or even most, of these children by name or by face, but they touched thousands with their deep caring, their singular sense of purpose, and their remarkable generosity.

Such, beyond the legend of Rockingham, is their legacy.

Mary Kuechenmeister

Table A

This table shows the amount of tax revenue from thoroughbred and harness racing and the General Fund Budget Appropriations for a given year. Tim Mason, administrative secretary for the Commissioners/Budget Office, provided the General Fund Budget Appropriation figures, which he compiled from the Revised Statutes Annotated (RSAs). The tax revenue figures for Thoroughbred Racing are taken from the Twelfth Annual Report of the New Hampshire Pari-Mutuel Commission, 1993. Figures for harness racing are taken from Kevin Cash's *A History of Rockingham Park*.

Year	Gen Fund Approps.	Tax Revenue/ Thoroughbreds	Tax Revenue/ Harness (begins in 1954)	% of Bd. Apprs.
1933	N\A	$416,693.26		
1934	$3,174,414	$656,629.74		20.68%
1935	$2,584,164	$395,898.02		15.3%
1936	$3,618,470	$350,543.76		9.6%
1937	$3,798,863	$612,910.21		16.1%
1938	$3,559,202	$380,523.81		10.69%
1939	$3,328,977	$619,930.03		18.62%
1940	N\A	$780,008.92		
1941	N\A	$1,004,803.39		
1942	N\A	$911,613.11		
1943	N\A	$1,206,674.51		
1944	$5,998,810	$1,714,459.70		28.57%
1945	$6,049,544	$2,649,791.40		43.8%
1946	$6,830,827	$3,193,931.37		46.75%
1947	$6,952,947	$2,710,280.16		38.98%
1948	$9,810,731	$2,666,859.63		27.18%
1949	$10,158,105	$1,937,240.86		19.07%
1950	$10,241,087	$1,759,395.77		17.17%
1951	$11,586,407	$2,069,377.56		17.86%
1952	$13,855,053	$2,418,352.23		17.45%
1953	$14,354,423	$2,528,491.16		17.61%
1954	$14,501,817	$2,146,039.78		14.79%
1955	$14,629,274	$2,418,320.89		16.53%
1956	$17,057,140	$2,811,657.65		16.48%
1957	$17,214,535	$3,169,332.10		18.41%
1958	$18,763,803	$3,052,605.55	$565,509.68	19.28%
1959	$19,329,399	$2,720,860.88	$934,233.77	18.90%
1960	$23,074,093	$3,163,290.33	$1,064,423.76	18.32%
1961	$23,936,897	$3,395,108.22	$1,318,891.77	19.69%
1962	$24,838,856	$3,403,123.17	$1,505,796.67	19.76%
1963	$26,112,189	$3,483,437.15	$1,731,228.10	19.97%
1964	$32,266,792	$4,527,586.00	$1,996,698.27	20.21%
1965	$33,172,165	$4,147,024.05	$2,284,559.43	19.38%
1966	$44,018,105	$4,206,048.52	$2,415,887.76	15.04%
1967	$43,284,339	$4,408,265.65	$2,253,749.30	15.39%
1968	$53,834,077	$4,432,647.71	$2,884,436.60	13.59%
1969	$57,145,954	$4,477,818.96	$2,811,270.48	12.75%
1970	$66,491,255	$5,674,049.35	$3,370,774.80	13.60%
1971	$71,810,432	$6,298,914.21	$3,459,166.86	13.58%
1972	$79,599,892	$5,236,744.07	$3,620,179.63	11.12%
1973	$82,114,459	$4,763,813.24	$3,287,806.45	9.80%
1974	$103,493,594	$4,546,406.48	$2,790,128.70	
1975	$109,349,575	$4,955,910.53	$2,044,609.25	

Endnotes

1. Pamphlet issued by the New England Racing Association. Found in the archives of Rockingham Park.

2. Telephone interview with Stewart Lamprey, New Hampshire House Speaker (1959-1965) and Senate President (1965-1970). April 20, 1997.

3. Telephone interview with Douglas Seed, Salem historian, July 16, 1996. See also Richard Noyes, *At the Edge of Megalopolis—A History of Salem, N.H., 1900-1974* (Canaan, N.H.: Phoenix Publishing, 1974).

4. Interview with Alan Pope, chief of staff to Govs. Lane Dwinell and Hugh Gregg. August 8, 1996.

5. Telephone interview with former House Ways and Means vice chair and Rockingham County Commissioner Ernie Barka. August 30, 1996.

6. *Report of Recess Tax Commission of 1927-28.* Commission members were: Milan A. Dickinson, Robert B. Hamblett, Roy D. Hunter, John W. Pearson, James P. Richardson, Sidney F. Stevens, Joseph O. Tremblay, Laurence F. Whittemore, and George H. Duncan. According to the report, 80 percent of all tax revenue was generated by property.

7. *Ibid.* Mr. Duncan dissented with the commission's recommendations.

8. "Breeders' Story Features Smith," *Manchester Union,* June 22, 1933.

9. See in general Howard G. Reynolds, "Liberal Purses for Rockingham," *Boston Sunday Post,* May 7, 1933.

10. *American Guide Series—New Hampshire: A Guide to the Granite State* (Boston: Houghton Mifflin Company, 1938), citing the U.S. Census at p. 8.

11. Bernard Bellush, *He Walked Alone—A Biography of John Gilbert Winant* (The Hague: Mouton & Co Printers, 1968) pp. 86, 87, 90, 92, and 101.

12. "Governor Silent on His Action on Racetrack Bill," *Manchester Leader,* April 1, 1933.

13. Kevin Cash, *Rockingham Park—A History* (Manchester: M.S. Walker, Inc., 1983) p. 26.

14. See in general Thomas E. Dewey, *Twenty Against the Under world* (Garden City, NY: Doubleday & Company, Inc., 1974).

15. Bernard Bellush, *He Walked Alone—A Biography of John Gilbert Winant* (The Hague: Mouton & Co, 1968), p. 92.

16. "Amoskeag Makes Loan of $500,000 to City at 6 PC"; "200 Strike at Quarries in Concord"; "Order Cutting Vets' Benefits Waits President's Signature"; and "Sheriff Fails to Reappoint Any Deputies," *Manchester Leader,* April 1, 1933 (front page).

17. Damon Runyon, "Ole Doc Runyon Goes Exploring in Granite State," *New York Press*, 1933. From the scrapbook of Louise Newman.

18. "Sportorials," *Lawrence Telegram*, May 23, 1933.

19. Telephone interview with Stewart Lamprey, New Hampshire House Speaker (1959-1965) and Senate President (1965-1970). April 20, 1997.

20. Twelfth Annual Report of the New Hampshire Pari-Mutuel Commission, 1993. See also Table A.

21. *Ibid.*

22. "Salem to Start Building at Once," *Manchester Leader*, April 4, 1933.

23. *Ibid.*

24. *Ibid.*

25. Howard G. Reynolds, "Horse Racing Is Expensive Sport," *Boston Sunday Post*, June 18, 1933.

26. "Rockingham Manager Talks at Rotary Club," *Lawrence Evening Tribune*, June 5, 1933.

27. "State Profits by Racing," *Transcript* (Peterborough), November 28, 1940.

28. Interview with Mike Dagostino Exeter, New Hampshire. May 2, 1996.

29. Arthur J. Conner, "A New State Highway," *Exeter News Letter*, April 29, 1938.

30. "New Road Job in Fall; Only War Will Stop It," *Lawrence Eagle-Tribune*, February 5, 1959.

31. Frederick W. Rovenkamp, "What Rockingham Track Did to Salem," *Rochester Courier*, November 3, 1955.

32. "New Route 93 to Save Time for Rockingham Park Patrons," *Lawrence Sunday Sun*, June 25, 1961.

33. "Smith Expands Parking Area at Rockingham," *Union Leader*, June 26, 1961.

34. "Board of Trade Guests Hear Rockingham Story," *Lawrence* (Mass.) *Evening Eagle-Tribune*, November 2, 1961.

35. "N.H. Jockey Club Is Salem's Top Taxpayer," *Lawrence Eagle-Tribune*, January 17, 1968.

36. *New Hampshire Jockey Club, Inc vs. Town of Salem*, Superior Court, September Term 1973 —E-2879, E-3724, E-4787, E-5884, E-7479. See also Richard Noyes, *At the Edge of Megalopolis—A History of Salem, N.H., 1900-1974* (Canaan, N.H.: Phoenix Publishing, 1974).

37. Ed Costello, "Many Share Windfall from Racetracks," *Boston Herald*, January 14, 1959.

38. Rockingham Park 1978 July 5 - September 17. Thoroughbred program guide published by track.

39. Telephone interview with Douglas Seed. July 16, 1996.

40. Telephone interview with Rockingham County Commissioner and former House Ways and Means vice chair Ernie Barka. August 30, 1996.

41. Interview with Mike Dagostino Exeter, New Hampshire. May 2, 1996.

42. "$150,000 Will Be Spent on Rockingham Improvements," *Manchester Union,* March 9, 1939.

43. Newspaper advertisement, *Lawrence Daily Eagle,* July 21, 1956, p. 7.

44. "Big Project at Rockingham," *Foster's Daily Democrat,* October 28, 1961.

45. "Big Expansion in Rock Plans," *Portland Press Herald,* February 4, 1961.

46. Noyes, *At the Edge of Megalopolis—A History of Salem, N.H., 1900-1974* (Canaan, N.H.: Phoenix Publishing, 1974) p. 512.

47. *New Hampshire State Year Book and Legislative Manual* (Portland, Maine: F Tower Companies, 1968).

48. "Rockingham Park Officials Sign Up with the N.R.A.," *Boston Herald* (?), September 7, 1933. From the press clipping books of Rockingham Park.

49. "New Hampshire Welfare Day! Monday, October Second, at Rockingham Park," *The Union* (Manchester), September 30, 1933. Fullpage ad.

50. "Fairs Battle Merrily for Racing Cash," *Concord Monitor,* November 21, 1940.

51. "State Helps NH Fairs Net $23,000," *Bennington* (Vt.) *Banner,* October 26, 1961.

52. In the press books of Rockingham Park a newspaper ad printed by Rockingham Park containing this information was found.

53. "State Revenue from Racetrack $2,512,102," *Portsmouth Herald,* July 8, 1938.

54. "State's Income Must Be Boosted to Pay Expenses," *Keene Sentinel,* May 16, 1941.

55. *Twelfth Annual Report of the New Hampshire Pari-Mutuel Commission, 1993,* State of New Hampshire.

56. "State's Income Must Be Boosted to Pay Expenses," *Keene Sentinel,* May 16, 1941.

57. "Racetrack Extension Bill Passed," *Manchester Leader,* June 5, 1941.

58. "Racetrack Extension," *Manchester Union,* May 19, 1941.

59. "Gambling Proposals In Spotlight," *Nashua Telegram,* March 14, 1941. See also "License More Gambling," *Granite State News* (Wolfboro), November 29, 1940.

60. "New Hampshire," *Boston Sunday Post,* August 14, 1955.

61. Leon W. Anderson, "The State Is My Beat," *Concord Monitor and New Hampshire Patriot,* May 13, 1958.

62. Leon W. Anderson, "The State Is My Beat," *Concord Monitor and New Hampshire Patriot,* April 2, 1958.

63. "Powell Bares Hold the Line Budget Plan," *Boston Herald,* March 11, 1959.

64. See Appendix A.

65. Telephone interview with Gov. Lane Dwinell. July 16, 1996.

66. Three flyers were found dating to 1937 and 1938 in the press clipping books at Rockingham Park. The flyers were no doubt used as a promotional piece. The General Court had to act on renewing the track's gambling license every two years.

67. Leon W Anderson, "The State Is My Beat," *Concord Monitor & New Hampshire Patriot,* July 20, 1956.

68. "Rock Gamblers Out of State," *Nashua Telegraph,* November 22, 1961.

69. "N.H. Thanks Bay State 'Sinners'," *Boston Record-American,* September 21, 1967.

70. *Ibid.*

71. Telephone interview with Gov. Lane Dwinell. July 16, 1996.

72. *Ibid.*

73. William Loeb, "Why a Sales Tax or Any New Taxes?" *Union Leader,* December 26, 1955.

74. Oliver Jenkins, "More Economy In Govt—N.H. Legislators to Study Streamlining of Departments," *Sunday Boston Herald,* February 8, 1959.

75. "We've Got Money Problems," *Berlin Reporter,* December 6, 1962.

76. *Ibid.*

77. Interview with Gov. Walter Peterson. January 28, 1997.

78. Leon W. Anderson, *To This Day the 300 Years of the New Hampshire Legislature* (Canaan, N.H.: Phoenix Publishing, 1981), p. 270.

79. Interview with Gov. Walter Peterson. January 28, 1997.

80. Leon W. Anderson, "The State Is My Beat," *Concord Monitor and New Hampshire Patriot,* July 16, 1969.

81. "For Uncle Lou, the Tributes Fly," *Union Leader,* April 21, 1969.

82. Dave Egan, "The Colonel Old Pioneer's New Frontier," *Boston Record,* July 19, 1956.

83. Telephone interview with Rockingham County Commissioner Ernie Barka. August 30, 1996.

84. Damon Runyon, "Lou Smith Cashes In on Personality to Score New Hampshire Racing Beat," *New York Press.* The article is not dated, but is likely to originate from the mid to late 1930s. It is taken from the scrapbook of Louise Newman. See also Eddie Hurley, "Easy to Win, Hard to Lose," *Boston Globe,* September 26, 1933.

85. This conclusion is based on a review of numerous articles written by Damon Runyon that extol the virtues of Lou Smith. A press packet issued by Rockingham Park in 1985 also references their strong friendship, which dates back to 1933. See also "A Tribute—Lou Smith," *Union Leader,* May 2, 1969.

86. Richard Noyes, *At the Edge of Megalopolis—A History of Salem, N.H., 1900-1974* (Canaan, N.H.: Phoenix Publishing, 1974) p. 199.

87. *Ibid,* p. 204.

88. Kevin Cash, *Rockingham Park—A History* (Manchester: M.S. Walker, Inc., 1983) p. 18.

89. Sam Cohen, "Rockingham's 'Mac' O'Dowd Dies at 79," *Boston Herald American,* October 25, 1973.

90. Brochure from the testimonial dinner honoring Richard M. O'Dowd. Pelham Inn, Pelham, New Hampshire. July 18, 1961.

91. "Dwinell Silent on Cotton Role in Allard Case," *New Hampshire Sunday News,* February 12, 1956.

92. Enoch Shenton, "Why County Officials Fight Reform to End Useless Layer of Government," *Franklin Journal-Transcript,* September 8, 1955.

93. "Report Atty Graf of Racetrack Counsel Urged for State Post," *Concord Monitor,* September 16, 1938.

94. "Attorney General Post to Phinney," *New Hampshire Sunday News,* March 13, 1949.

95. "Big U.S. Job to Phinney," *New Hampshire Sunday News,* July 10, 1955.

96. *Ibid.*

97. "Candidates Invited to Visit Rockingham," *Haverhill* (Mass.)*Gazette,* October 3, 1938.

98. "Cheney Links Murphy with Salem Track," *Concord Monitor,* September 12, 1938. See also "Cheney Looks for Victory," *Manchester Union,* September 12, 1938, and "Governor Never Visited Track," *Laconia Citizen,* September 10, 1938.

99. "Rockingham Head Denies Charges Large Sums Are Spent to Win Advantages," *Haverhill* (Mass.) *Gazette* September 8, 1938.

100. "Racetrack Never Seen by Murphy," *Boston Post,* September 9, 1938.

101. "N.H. Track Head Blames Politics," *Boston Herald,* September 9, 1938.

102. "Rockingham Park Bettors Will Not Pay 'Breakage'," *Springfield* (Mass.) *Union,* July 6, 1938.

103. "Rockingham Park in Plea for 'Breakage' to Stay Alive," *Boston Herald,* March 28, 1963.

104. "Racing Probe Is Rejected by Solons after a Hearing," *Dover Democrat,* January 19, 1939. See also "Representatives Attack, Defend Probe of Racing," *Claremont Eagle,* January 17, 1939.

105. "Allege $100,000 Spent by Track for 'Good-Will'," *Lynn* (Mass.) *Item,* September 8, 1938.

106. "Rockingham Head Denies Charges Large Sums Are Spent to Win Advantages," *Haverhill Gazette,* September 8, 1938.

107. "Solons Get Jobs at Rockingham," *Leader* (Manchester), August 1, 1940.

108. James Stack, "Senator Cotton Aided Allard to Race Board," *New Hampshire Sunday News,* February 5, 1956.

109. D. Frank O'Neil, "Governor Calls Probe of Track Very Desirable," *Union Leader,* August 20, 1955.

110. "11,743,326 Persons Have Attended Race Programs at Rock (in 23 Yrs)," *New Hampshire Sunday News,* July 15, 1956.

111. "Honor Official N.H. Jockey Club," *Foster's Democrat and Enquirer,* May 28, 1959.

112. Interview with Alan Pope Portsmouth, New Hampshire. August 8, 1996.

113. "Mayors Meet Here," *Nashua Telegraph,* August 1, 1956.

114. Leon W. Anderson, "The State Is My Beat," *Concord Monitor & New Hampshire Patriot*, April 11, 1958.

115. Tom Henshaw, "New Hampshire: What Presidential Aspirants See In It," *New Bedford* (Mass.)*Standard Times,* March 1, 1964.

116. "N.H. Legislators Slash Spending to Prevent $3,000,000 Deficit," *Boston Herald,* July 17, 1949.

117. "N.H. Lottery Voted," *Christian Science Monitor,* August 5, 1955.

118. Telephone interview with Stewart Lamprey, House Speaker (1959-1965) and Senate President (1965- 1970). April 20, 1997.

119. "N.H. Lottery Voted," *Christian Science Monitor,* August 5, 1955.

120. Telephone interview with Gov. Lane Dwinell, July 16, 1996.

121. *Ibid.*

122. Telephone interview with Stewart Lamprey, House Speaker (1959-1965) and Senate President (1965- 1970). April 20, 1997.

123. Interview with Gov. Hugh Gregg. Nashua, New Hampshire. January 25, 1996.

124. *Ibid.*

125. Interview with Gov. Walter Peterson. January 28, 1997.

126. Telephone interview with Gov. Lane Dwinell. July 16, 1996.

127. Rockingham Park 1978: July 5 - September 17 Thoroughbred program from Rockingham Park.

128. Telephone interview with Gov. Lane Dwinell. July 16, 1996.

129. Telephone interview with Stewart Lamprey, House Speaker (1959-1965) and Senate President (1965- 1970). April 20, 1997.

130. *Ibid.*

131. Interview with Atty. Robert A. Shaines. Portsmouth, New Hampshire. August 8, 1996.

132. Walter O. Pennell, "Sidelights from the State House," *News Letter* (Exeter), January 30, 1941.

133. "Lou Smith Denies Church Charges—Rockingham Magnate Answers 'Social Action' Prober," *Lowell* (Mass.) *Sun,* September 8, 1938.

134. "Drive to Organize Racetrack Employees," *Union Leader*, September 2, 1955.

135. Dick Wagner, "The Sport Scene," *Berlin Reporter*, August 30, 1967.

136. Telephone interview with Stewart Lamprey House Speaker (1959-1965) and Senate President (1965- 1970). April 20, 1997.

137. Interview with Mike Dagostino Exeter, New Hampshire. May 2, 1996.

138. Interview with Gov. Walter Peterson. January 28, 1997.

139. *Ibid.*

140. "Baptist Meet In Rochester," *Union* (Manchester), May 5, 1938.

141. "N.H. Congregationalists to Fight Legalized Betting," *Leader* (Manchester), May 17, 1938. See also, "Churchmen Announce War on Gambling," *Concord Monitor*, May 17, 1936.

142. "Lou Smith Denies Church Charges—Rockingham Magnate Answers 'Social Action' Prober," *Lowell* (Mass.) *Sun*, September 8, 1938. See also "Salem Track Linked to Dewey Racket Probe; See "Race Money Used to 'Political Advantage'," *Keene Sentinel*, September 9, 1938.

143. "Hines on Rockingham Track Payroll 5 Years, Report Reveals," *Concord Monitor*, March 24, 1939. See also "N.H. Racetrack Officials Not Getting Into Wrangle," *Foster's Democrat*, September 8, 1938.

144. "Committee Launches Study of Rockingham's Finances Before Voting on License," *Concord Monitor*, February 1, 1939.

145. "News from the State Capital," *Milford* (N.H.) *Cabinet*, February 2, 1939.

146. "Committee Votes 19 to 4 Favor of Pari-Mutuel Bill," *Keene Sentinel*, February 7, 1939. See also "Record Revenue from Racetrack," *Manchester Union*, December 4, 1940.

147. "Boost 'Cut' at Salem Track," *Boston Post*, February 15, 1939.

148. "Boost State Tax on Pools to Four Per Cent," *Manchester Union*, February 15, 1939.

149. "Senate Passes Racetrack Betting Bill," *Rochester* (N.H.) *Courier*, February 23, 1939.

150. "Barron Measure Wins in Senate by 13-10 Vote," *Manchester Union*, February 23, 1939.

151. "Senate, House Approve Bill, As Amended," *Manchester Leader*, March 7, 1939.

152. D. Frank O'Neil, "Under the State House Dome," *Morning Union Leader*, March 16, 1967.

153. "Would Tax Hike At Rock Scare Big Bettors?" *Keene Sentinel*, February 26, 1959.

154. "Board of Trade Guests Hear Rockingham Story," *Lawrence Evening Eagle-Tribune*, November 2, 1961.

155. Eddie Hurley, "Personal Triumph for Lou Smith," *Daily Record* (?) 1933 or 1934 (?) From the scrapbook of Louise Newman.

156. "Race Commission Opens Up Stock List," *Portsmouth Herald*, March 23, 1968.

157. "Discusses Rockingham," *Lawrence* (Mass.) *Tribune,* May 25, 1956, and John R. Aborn, "DeSpirito Lauds His Boss," *Providence* (RI) *Journal,* April 26, 1956.

158. Press packet issued by Rockingham Park, April 2, 1985.

159. "Nip Plot on Lou Smith," From the scrapbook of Louise Newman. The article appears to date back to the 1930s. Neither a date nor the paper of origin are visible.

160. Interview with Gov. Hugh Gregg. Nashua, New Hampshire. January 25, 1996.

161. "N.H. Court Rules Tack Can Bar 'Undesirables'," *Greenfield* (Mass.) *Recorder-Gazette,* July 18, 1960.

162. "Supreme Court Upholds Ban of Pair from Rock," *Laconia Citizen,* July 20, 1960.

163. "Says 'Rock' Has State 'By Throat'," *Boston Post,* January 27, 1949.

164. "Says Track Has N.H. 'By Throat'," *Boston Globe,* January 27, 1949.

165. "N.H. House OK's 'Rock' Extension," *Lawrence Tribune,* February 9, 1949.

166. "Churches Plan 'United Front' in Racetrack," *Claremont Eagle,* January 22, 1949.

167. Frederick W. Rovenkamp, "What Rockingham Track Did to Salem," *Rochester Courier,* November 3, 1955.

168. *Ibid.*

169. "Track to Get Long Tenure," *Concord Monitor,* January 27, 1949.

170. "Tells Baptist Women How to Kill Gambling," *Foster's Democrat,* May 18, 1938.

171. "Opposed to Racetrack Gambling," *Manchester Leader,* October 7, 1938.

172. "Salem Pari-Mutuel Betting Condemned by Methodists," *Manchester Leader,* April 22, 1938.

173. "N.H. Universalists Oppose Gambling at Rack Track," *Manchester Union,* September 13, 1938.

174. "Hancock Minister Says He Believes Racetrack Is Detrimental to State," *Keene Sentinel,* September 10, 1938.

175. "Civic League Prepared for Racing Battle," *Concord Monitor,* June 1, 1938.

176. "Oppose Racetrack Renewal," *Nashua Telegraph,* June 24, 1938.

177. "Oppose Salem Track License," *Union,* May 26, 1938.

178. Leon W. Anderson, "The State Is My Beat," *Monitor & New Hampshire Patriot,* February 3, 1956.

179. Jack Kane, "Rockingham Track Out to Protect Interests; Faces Many Problems," *New Hampshire Sunday News,* February 8, 1959.

180. Herb Ralby, "$50,000 Dog Race Seen as Sport Keeps Growing," *Boston Morning Globe,* July 23, 1956.

181. "New Hampshire Groups Clash Over Dog Racing," *Boston Herald,* February 12, 1959.

182. Bob Norling, "Rough Going for Dogs at Debate on Bill," *Portsmouth Herald*, February 12, 1959.

183. *Ibid.*

184. "Unholy Alliance Charge by Dog Racing Backer," *Union Leader*, March 24, 1959.

185. Frank D. O'Neil, "Under the State House Dome," *Union Leader*, February 14, 1959.

186. Interview with Atty. Robert A. Shaines. Portsmouth, New Hampshire. August 8, 1996.

187. "As We See It—Thumbs Down On Greyhound Racing," *News & New Boston Times*, Goffstown (N.H.), February 19, 1959.

188. "House Kills Proposals On Greyhound Betting," *Lebanon* (N.H.) *Valley News*, March 25, 1959.

189. "Scamman Says Rock Controls Gambling Vote," *Haverhill* (Mass.) *Gazette*, May 1, 1958.

190. Interview with Atty. Robert A. Shaines. Portsmouth, New Hampshire. August 8, 1996.

191. *Ibid.*

192. "Horses vs Dogs In New Hampshire," *Worcester Telegram & Gazette*, February 20, 1959.

193. Interview with Atty. Robert A. Shaines. Portsmouth, New Hampshire. August 8, 1996.

194. Interview with Gov. Walter Peterson. January 28, 1997.

195. "N.H. Sweeps Bills Gets Further Study," *Boston American*, February 25, 1959.

196. Website, The Granite State's Lottery—New Hampshire's Sweepstakes Commission, January 30, 1998, www.state.nh.us/lottery/history.htm. See also, "N.H. Lottery Voted," *Christian Science Monitor*, August 5, 1955. Actually, the first state to pass a lottery was Louisiana, but it abandoned the lottery in 1892.

197. John R. Aborn, "N.H. May Change Lottery Format in 1968," *Providence* (R.I.) *Bulletin*, July 31, 1967.

198. Gordon A. Glover, "New Hampshire Only State with Legal Sweepstakes," *Newport* (Vt.) *Express*, May 1, 1963.

199. "Proposed N.H. Sweepstakes Plan Snagged," *Taunton* (Mass.) *Gazette*, February 5, 1959.

200. "Sweepstakes Spur for Rock Trots?" *Boston Evening Globe*, March 12, 1964.

201. John R. Aborn, "Lou the Umbrella Man 'Sweeps' Horses," *Providence* (R.I.) *Bulletin*, March 31, 1964.

202. "Sweepstakes Pace Planned Next May at Rockingham," *Citizen Laconia*, December 22, 1967.

108   E N D N O T E S

203. Telephone interview with historian Douglas Seed, Salem, New Hampshire. July 16, 1996.

204. Interview with Mike Dagostino, personnel manager at Rockingham Park. Exeter, New Hampshire. May 2, 1996.

205. Interview with Louise Newman, secretary to Lou Smith. Portsmouth, New Hampshire. November 16, 1995.

206. Telephone interview with Rockingham County Commissioner and former House Ways and Means vice chair Ernie Barka. August 30, 1996.

207. W.P. Peters, "Ponies Are Coming Back to Salem for the Third Time," *Lawrence Evening Tribune,* June 19, 1933.

208. George Holland, "20,000 Expected at Rockingham," *Boston Daily Record,* June 21, 1933.

209. "20,000 Crowd Inspects Rockingham Racetrack," *Manchester Union,* June 19, 1933.

210. George Holland, "20,000 Expected at Rockingham," *Boston Daily Record,* June 21, 1933.

211. Interview with Mike Dagostino. Exeter, New Hampshire, May 2, 1996.

212. "Celebrities Attend Wynn Play Opening," *Boston Sunday Advertiser,* October 31, 1937, and "A Day at the Races," *Boston Evening American,* October 30, 1937.

213. Interview with Louise Newman, secretary to Lou Smith. Portsmouth, New Hampshire. November 16, 1995.

214. Interview with Mike Dagostino. Exeter, New Hampshire. May 2, 1996.

215. "2 Jockeys Hurt In Rockingham Steeplechase," *Boston Daily Record,* September, 1933. From the scrapbooks of Rockingham Park. See also Eddie Hurley, "Juveniles Face Barrier—Bangtails Attracted U.S. Senator David I. Walsh," *Boston Daily Record,* September 11, 1933, and "Sen. Bridges Relaxes at Racetrack," *Manchester Leader,* October 1, 1938.

216. "Sen Bridges Relaxes at Racetrack," *Manchester Leader,* October 1, 1938.

217. Pres Hobson, "Madden Most Unusual Racing Commissioner," *Quincy* (Mass.) *Patriot-Ledger,* September 27, 1962.

218. Telephone interview with Nackey Loeb. January 11, 1996.

219. Leon W. Anderson, "The State Is My Beat," *Concord Monitor & Patriot,* May 11, 1960.

220. Interview with Gov. Hugh Gregg. Nashua, New Hampshire. January 25, 1996.

221. Bob Hilliard, "The Sports Desk—Lou Smith Touch Brings Success to Rockingham," *New Hampshire Sunday News,* April 16, 1967.

222. "MacPhail Is Visitor Here," *New Bedford* (Mass.) *Standard-Times,* July 28, 1956.

223. "Royalty at Rock Tuesday," *New Hampshire Sunday News,* April 14, 1963. See also "Royal Visitor Feted," *Boston Record-American,* April 17, 1963.

224. *Ibid.*

225. "To Be Honored—Eileen Farrell," *Nashua Telegraph,* April 22, 1969.

226. Mary Fitzgerald, "The Aura of the Rich and Famous Rose from Rockingham's Flames," *Lawrence Eagle-Tribune,* July 29, 1980.

227. "Holovak Joins Guests Honored by B'nai B'rith," *Boston Record-American,* December 5, 1962. See also "Stars Gather Here for B'nai B'rith," *Boston Sunday Advertiser,* December 9, 1962.

228. George W. Clarke, *Boston Sunday Advertiser,* August (?) 1951.

229. George W. Clarke, "All the Familiar Faces Seen at Track Opening," *Boston Record,* May 16, 1956.

230. Dorothy Patten, "Mrs Louis Smith of Salem—Woman with a Cause," *Haverhill Gazette,* March 31, 1967.

231. "Red Cross Day at Rockingham," *Boston Post,* August 31, 1955.

232. Ed Gallagher, "A Tribute—Lou Smith," *Union Leader,* May 2, 1969.

233. Telephone interview with Rockingham County Commissioner Ernie Barka. August 30, 1996.

234. Interview with Mike Dagostino. Exeter, New Hampshire. May 2, 1996.

235. "Gift to Rockingham Park," *Woburn* (Mass.) *Telegram,* January 15, 1960.

236. "Rockingham Park Charity Distribution," *Coos County Democrat,* January 7, 1959.

237. Charlie Kelley, "Aunt Lutza Beneficent," *Boston American,* July 22, 1961.

238. "Cushing to Offer Mass at Racetrack Charity Bake," *Newburyport* (Mass.) *News,* August 9, 1949.

239. George Clarke, "Around Boston—$100,000 Lures Big Stars Here," *Boston Record,* May 21, 1960.

240. Telephone interview with former House Ways and Means vice chair and Rockingham County Commissioner Ernie Barka. August 30, 1996.

241. Sam Cohen, "They Live for the Children of Others," *Boston Sunday Advertiser,* December 25, 1955.

242. *Ibid.*

243. Vic Emanual, "Meet Mrs Lou Smith, Wife of the Epsom Downs Boss," *Houston Post*, December 31, 1933.

244. Dorothy Patten, "Mrs Louis Smith of Salem—Woman with a Cause," *Haverhill Gazette,* March 31, 1967.

245. "Record Crowd on Hand for Aunt Lutza's Charity Luncheon at Rock," *Derry* (N.H.) *Enterprise*, August 3, 1960.

246. Interview with Louise Newman, secretary to Lou Smith. November 16, 1995.

247. Interview with Mike Dagostino. Exeter, New Hampshire. May 2, 1996.

248. George W. Clarke, "Around Boston," *Boston Daily Record,* August 5, 1951, and August 26, 1949. The celebration of Mass started in 1947 when the track was gripped by "swamp fever" and horsemen needed spiritual sustenance. Father Pat Kenneally of St. Joseph's Church in Salem held the first service.

249. See in general "Archbishop at Rockingham," *Boston Evening American,* August 29, 1949.

250. "3,800 Delegates Expected Here for CWV Convention," *Union Leader,* August 14, 1956.

251. "Kennedy Memorial Gets $70,000 Donation," *Allston Brighton Citizen Item,* November 25, 1976.

252. D. Frank O'Neil, "Under the State House Dome," *Union Leader,* April 23, 1969.

253. Sam Cohen, "They Live for the Children of Others," *Boston Sunday Advertiser,* December 25, 1955. See also "Annual Christmas Party Big Success," *Boston Record,* December 23, 1955, and "Bring Cheer to Kennedy Memorial Children," *Lawrence Tribune,* December 23, 1955.

254. "Pony Ride," *Boston Record,* May 14, 1956.

255. Sam Cohen, "They Live for the Children of Others," *Boston Sunday Advertiser,* December 25, 1955.

256. *Ibid.*

257. "Track to Get Long Tenure," *Concord Monitor,* January 27, 1949.

258. Norma Sherburne, " 'Bet a 100 Right On the Nose' Orders 'Rack Track' Lou: Most Famous of Women Bettors at Rockingham Park," *Boston Herald,* September 8, 1933.

259. "Lady in Red Bets $21,000, NJ Track Is Minus $47,000," *Boston Traveler,* August 17, 1949.

260. Norma Sherburne, "'Bet a 100 Right On the Nose' Orders 'Rack Track' Lou: Most Famous of Women Bettors at Rockingham Park," *Boston Herald,* September 8, 1933.

261. "Offer Style Tips on Track Fashions," *New Hampshire Sunday News,* July 15, 1956.

262. *Ibid.*

263. *Ibid.*

264. Bowdoin Plumer, "The People's Forum," *Bristol* (N.H.) *Enterprise,* December 3, 1959.

265. "Work Begins at 'Old Rock' for Summer Meet," *Concord Monitor,* May 24, 1938.

266. "Turn Verein to Repeat Show—Capacity Audience Enjoys Premiere of 'Rockingham,' " *Leader* (Manchester), April 26, 1938.

267. "A Tribute—Lou Smith," *Union Leader,* May 2, 1969.

268. Interview with Mike Dagostino Exeter, New Hampshire. May 2, 1996.

269. George Clarke, "Around Boston—'Stuff That Dreams Are Made Of,' " *Boston Record*, April 16, 1960.

270. "Aluminum Will Be Collected Here Tomorrow," *Concord Monitor*, July 21, 1941.

271. "Rockingham Opens Monday— 'Aluminum Day' to Mark First Day of Summer Meet," *Manchester Union*, July 19, 1941.

272. Interview with Mike Dagostino Exeter, New Hampshire. May 2, 1996.

273. *Ibid.*

274. *Ibid.*

275. "Young Rail Birds," *Leader*, July 12, 1936.

276. "Rockingham's Glad Hand!" *Boston Post*, July 12, 1938.

277. "Boyington Here Today to Autograph Books," *Boston Herald*, May 7, 1959.

278. "Pope, President Have N.E. Track Gimmicks," *Providence* (R.I.) *Bulletin*, January 7, 1965.

279. Interview with Gov. Hugh Gregg. Nashua, New Hampshire. January 25, 1996.

280. "Lou Smith Is Whooping It Up for Red Sox," *Claremont* (N.H.) *Eagle*, September 29, 1949.

281. According to a Certificate of Naturalization (No. 5384200) in the possession of Louise Newman, Lou Smith became a U.S. citizen on August 31, 1942. The certificate was executed in Rockingham Superior Court and lists Lou Smith's former nationality as British.

282. Interview with Louise Newman, secretary to Lou Smith. November 16, 1995.

283. "Final Rites Held for Lou Smith, Pioneer of New England Racing," *Morning Telegraph*, April 22, 1969.

284. Damon Runyon, "Lou Smith Cashes In on Personality to Score New Hampshire Racing Beat," *New York Press*, May 3, 1933.

285. "Over 500 Attend Lou Smith Rites," *Lawrence* (Mass.) *Eagle-Tribune*, April 22, 1969.

286. "Smith Ends Last Race," *Haverhill* (Mass.) *Gazette*, April 22, 1969.

287. Eddie Hurley, "A Day in 1931, Now Smith Smiles," *Boston Daily Record* (?) June 8, 1935.

288. Eddie Hurley, "Smith to Put Cuba on Map," *Boston Daily Record* (?), October 11, 1937. From the scrapbook of Louise Newman. See also Sam Cohen, "Jim Munroe Signs with Smith as Havana Track Race Secretary," *Boston Sunday Advertiser*, October 31, 1937.

289. *Ibid.*

290. "Dempsey Cuts Loose in Praise of Epsom Downs," *Collyer's Eye & Baseball World*, Vol 19, No. 33, November 11, 1933.

291. "200 Houstonians Get Work So Racetrack Can Open," *Houston Chronicle,* November 30, 1933.

292. "Governor to Attend Epsom Downs Opener," *Houston Chronicle,* November 20, 1933.

293. "Green Tree Stable Will Race at Epsom Downs Inaugural Meet—C.V. Whitney Wires for 16 Stables," *Houston Post,* October 31, 1933.

294. Lloyd Gregory, "Manager Lou Smith Says $600,000 Race Plant Will Be Ready November 25," *Houston Post,* November 14, 1933.

295. "Lou Smith—Has 50 Years of Experience in Racetracks," *Las Vegas Review-Journal,* September 4, 1953.

296. Frank Wright, curator of manuscripts for the Nevada State Museum and Historical Society, researched this topic after a phone inquiry for a radio script for a local PBS station. He provided a copy of the script to the author in a letter dated 23 March 1998.

297. *Ibid.* See also "Al Luke Promoter of Plan to Salvage Las Vegas Track," *Las Vegas Review-Journal,* September 4, 1953.

298. *Ibid.*

299. "Final Rites Held for Lou Smith, Pioneer of New England Racing," *Morning Telegraph,* April 22, 1969.

300. Interview with Alan Pope, chief of staff to Govs. Lane Dwinell and Hugh Gregg. Portsmouth, New Hampshire. August 8, 1996.

301. "Lou Smith," *Boston Herald,* January 23, 1956.

302. Joe Barnea, "Barnstorming with Barnea," *Union Leader,* April 22, 1969.

303. "Rock Pace Honors Lou Smith," *Boston Sunday Advertiser,* September 18, 1960.

304. "New Hampshire Well Represented at Dedication of Lou-Lutza Smith Wing of Kennedy Memorial," *Derry News & Salem Enterprise,* October 12, 1961.

305. Interview with Mike Dagostino. Exeter, New Hampshire. May 2, 1996.

306. Bob Hilliard, "The Sports Desk—Lou Smith Touch Brings Success to Rockingham," *New Hampshire Sunday News,"* April 16, 1967.

307. Interview with Louise Newman, secretary to Lou Smith. Portsmouth, New Hampshire. November 16, 1995.

308. *Ibid.*

309. Telephone interview with former House Ways and Means vice chair and Rockingham County Commissioner Ernie Barka. August 30, 1996.

310. Telephone interview with Stewart Lamprey, House Speaker (1959-1965) and Senate President (1965- 1970). April 20, 1997.

311. Leo Cloutier, "Graf, O'Dowd Topnotch to Operate Ole Rock," *Peterborough Transcript,* June 5, 1969.

312. "For Uncle Lou, the Tributes Fly," *Union Leader,* April 21, 1969.

313. "Over 500 Attend Lou Smith Rites," *Lawrence Eagle-Tribune*, April 22, 1969.

314. "Final Rites Held for Lou Smith, Pioneer of New England Racing," *Morning* (N.H.) *Telegraph*, April 22, 1969.

315. *Ibid.*

316. "Final Tribute Paid Lou Smith," *Haverhill* (Mass.) *Gazette*, April 22,1969.

317. "For Uncle Lou, the Tributes Fly," *Union Leader*, April 21, 1969.

318. *Ibid.*

319. Interview with Gov. Hugh Gregg. Nashua, New Hampshire. January 25, 1996.

320. Interview with Gov. Walter Peterson. January 28, 1997.

321. Interview with Louise Newman, secretary to Lou Smith. Portsmouth, New Hampshire. November 16, 1995.

322. Interview with Alan Pope, chief of staff to Govs. Lane Dwinell and Hugh Gregg. August 8, 1996.

323. Interview with Mike Dagostino. Exeter, New Hampshire. May 2, 1996.

324. Interview with Edward Callahan. Current general manager for Rockingham Park. Salem, New Hampshire. June 29, 1996.

325. P.J. Cullen, "Reservist Lone Favorite to Win in Seven-Race Program at Rockingham," *Boston Herald*, June 30, 1933.

326. Lou Najac, "Rockingham Park Opens Fall Meet," *Post*, September 4, 1933. From a 1933 press clipping book kept by Rockingham Park. But Howard G. Reynolds, "Horse Racing Is Expensive Sport," *Boston Sunday Post*, June 18, 1933, places the worth of the horses at $1 million.

327. John Barry "Rockingham Park Race Meet Opens Tomorrow Afternoon," *Boston Globe*, June 20, 1933.

328. *Rockingham Park 1978—July 5-September 17.* Racing program published by Rockingham Park.

329. "Great Horses Going to Post In Big Stakes," *Boston Globe*, August 31, 1933

330. Arthur Siegel, "15-Yr-Old Dominates Meet Before 12,000," *Boston Herald*, September 3, 1933.

331. W.P. Peters "Ensor Has Mount on Three Winners at Rockingham, " *Lawrence Daily Eagle*, June 22, 1933.

332. "$180,700 In Purses at Rockingham—Seabiscuit to Compete in 24-Day Meet," *Boston Evening American*, September 17, 1937.

333. "Rockingham's Feature Race Attracts Stars," *Milford* (Mass.) *News*, July 21, 1938.

334. "Rockingham Opening Attracts $15,000," *Manchester Union*, July 25, 1939.

335. "Memories Galore Make a Lifetime of Thrills," *Boston Sunday Advertiser*, July 28, 1968.

336. "Winningest Jockey in History at Rock," *Salem Observer,* June 28, 1977.

337. *50th Anniversary—Rockingham Park—Press Guide—April 19-November 24, 1985.* From the archives of Rockingham Park. See also Larry Claflin, "One That Got Away Still Haunts Shoe," *Boston Herald American*, July 6, 1977. See also "Top Jockeys at Rockingham for NE Futurity Wednesday," *New Hampshire Sunday News*, August 27, 1961.

338. "Tony DeSpirito Very Definitely Plans to Resume Riding Again," *Manchester Union Leader,* November 24, 1955.

339. "Whitney Stable at Rockingham—Col. Bradley Also to Have Horses at Salem Track," *Union* (Manchester), June 2, 1938.

340. "Louis Mayer Ships Horses to Rockingham," *Nashua Telegraph,* July 18, 1939.

341. Dave Wilson, "Rockingham Park Opening Tomorrow Looms as Top 18-Day Race Meeting under Lou Smith," *Boston Advertiser,* July 10, 1938.

342. "Mgr. Lou Smith Eliminates Post Parades at Rockingham," *Manchester Union,* October 31, 1940.

343. "Closed Circuit TV for Patrons at Rockingham," *Union Leader,* April 13, 1959.

344. "Lou's New Surrey," *Chelsea* (Mass.) *Record*, July 8, 1960.

345. Bob Waldo, "Pic-Six Catching On at Rockingham," *Boston Sunday Advertiser,* July 17, 1960.

346. "Rocking Horse Park Popular with Children," *New Hampshire Sunday News*, July 15, 1956.

347. John R. Aborn, "All-2-Year-Old Card Big Success at 'Rock'," *Providence* (R.I.) *Journal*, September 28, 1955.

348. Dave Egan, "Rock Owner Emphasizes Young Stock," *Lebanon Valley News,* September 28, 1955.

349. "Thousands of Dollars Yearly for Charities," *Union Leader,* June 30, 1967.

350. "1400 Thoroughbreds Set for 35th Rock Opening," *Sunday Boston Globe,* July 2, 1967.

351. Bob Hilliard, "The Sports Desk—Fall Harness Meeting Sets 'Rock' Records In Spite of Red Sox," *New Hampshire Sunday News,* November 5, 1967.

352. Baseball Encyclopedia (New York: Macmillan Publishing, 1993).

353. Bob Hilliard, "The Sports Desk—Fall Harness Meeting Sets 'Rock' Records In Spite of Red Sox," *New Hampshire Sunday News,* November 5, 1967.

354. "Canadian, New Zealand Pacers in Rock Feature," *Boston Record-American,* February 22, 1969.

355. "Top Horses Set for Rock Meet," *Evening Union Leader,* September 1, 1961.

356. "Rock Sulkies Go Friday; Nation's Top Drivers Vie," *Boston Sunday Advertiser,* September 3, 1961.

357. "N.H. Gets $1.6M from Rockingham," *Claremont Eagle,* May 13, 1966.

358. "13,791 See Trotters," *Lowell* (Mass.) *Sun,* April 2, 1960.

359. Owen Flynn, "Record Mile at Rock," *Lowell Sun,* April 16, 1960.

360. "Isles of Shoals Pace Tonight at Rockingham," *Morning Union Leader,* May 6, 1961.

361. "Unbeaten Trotter from Canada Races Tonight," *Attleboro* (Mass.) *Sun,* April 7, 1967.

362. "Scottish Design Draws the Rail in Tonight's Rock Hampton Pace," *Lebanon Valley* (N.H.) *News,* May 6, 1967.

363. "World Champion Pacer Skipper Gene in Atlantic Seaboard Pace," *Lawrence Sunday Sun,* September 18, 1966.

364. "Woman Driver to Be Back at Rock," *Haverhill* (Mass.) *Journal,* January 30, 1961.

365. Ike Isaacson, "All Around Town," *Foster's Democrat,* April 12, 1960.

366. "Miss Huntress to Drive in Harness Meet At 'Rock,'" *Haverhill* (Mass.) *Gazette,* September 5, 1961.

367. "Turf History to be Written by Rockingham," *Dover Democrat,* August 9, 1949. See in general, "Salem Track to Slash Its Staff 20 PC," *Concord Monitor,* August 13, 1949.

368. Dave Wilson, "Smith Can Be Proud of New England Futurity," *Boston American,* September 16, 1955.

369. "New Sulky Race System Debuts Friday at Rock," *Marlboro* (Mass.) *Enterprise,* March 11, 1963.

370. Gennaro King Costantino, *Gazzetta del Massachusetts,* July 20, 1956 (English language ethnic newspaper). Clipping found in press book at Rockingham Park.

371. "National Horsemen's Group Born 20 Years Ago at Rock," *Derry* (N.H.) *Enterprise,* July 19, 1960.

372. "New Face On Old Rock," *Boston Record,* August 3, 1949.

373. Interview with Edward Callahan. Salem, New Hampshire. June 29, 1996.

374. *Ibid.*

375. Dave Egan, "The Colonel Old Pioneer's New Frontier," *Boston Record,* July 19, 1956.

376. "Big Opening Monday for Streamlined 'Rock'," *Lawrence* (Mass.) *Eagle-Tribune,* July 20, 1956.

377. Leon W. Anderson, "The State Is My Beat," *Concord Monitor & Patriot,* July 20, 1956.

378. Tom Kenney, "Sports Talk—Billy Whalen Great Catching Prospect," *Malden* (Mass.) *Evening News,* July 27, 1956.

379. "Big Opening Monday for Streamlined 'Rock'," *Lawrence* (Mass.) *Eagle Tribune*, July 20, 1956.

380. "Stylish Rock Open to Public on Sunday," *Boston Record*, July 21, 1956.

381. Jack McGrath, "A Bit of This and a Bit of That," *Troy* (N.Y.) *Times Record*, July 18, 1956.

382. Interview with Louise Newman, secretary to Lou Smith. Portsmouth, New Hampshire. November 16, 1995.

383. Interview with Alan Pope. Chief of staff to Governors Lane Dwinell and Hugh Gregg. Portsmouth, New Hampshire. August 8, 1996.

384. Interview with Atty. Robert A. Shaines. Portsmouth, New Hampshire. August 8, 1996.

385. "Racing's Slump Laid to Veeck," *Providence* (R.I.) *Evening Bulletin*, February 26, 1973.

386. *Ibid.*

387. "Compromise May End Threat of Race War," *Beverly* (Mass.) *Times*, March 9, 1938.

388. See in general Austen Lake, "How to Avoid Horrors of a Racetrack War," *Boston Evening American*, January 28, 1948.

389. Jack Kane, "Rockingham Track Out to Protect Interests; Faces Many Problems," *New Hampshire Sunday News*, February 8, 1959.

390. "Horse Track War Looms as Result of Demands of Dario," *Gazzetta del Massachusetts*, December 24, 1955.

391. Huck Finnegan, "Dario Demands Summit Meeting," *Boston Daily Record-American*, March 13, 1962.

392. "N.H., R.I. Track 'War' Threatened," *Manchester Evening Union Leader*, February 20, 1962.

393. Jack Kane, "Rockingham Park, First New England Track Is Still Rated as Finest," *New Hampshire Sunday News*, April 1, 1962.

394. Interview with Mike Dagostino. Exeter, New Hampshire. May 2, 1996.

395. "Lou Smith's Using 'Pressure'—Rizzo," *Morning Eagle-Tribune*, February 26, 1968.

396. Russ Conway, "Rock Bids for Smaller Revenue State Bite," *Lawrence Eagle-Tribune*, May 28, 1973.

397. *Ibid.*

398. William Loeb, "Let's Look Under the 'Rock' "—editorial, *Manchester Union Leader*, May 9, 1973.

399. "Rockingham Park: Now Just a Choice Piece of Property?" *New England Business*, Vol. 2, No. 14, September 1, 1980.

400. "All Bets Are Off," *Boston Globe*, July 30, 1980.

401. "Rockingham Park: Now Just a Choice Piece of Property?" *New England Business*, Vol. 2, No. 14, September 1, 1980.

402. *Ibid.*

403. Chris Woodward, "Loss of Track's Income Will Hurt Salem," *Lawrence Eagle-Tribune*, July 29, 1980.

404. Russ Conway and Kathie Neff, " 'Rock' Target: Aug 8; No State Aid Coming," *Lawrence Eagle-Tribune*, July 30, 1980.

405. Press packet from Rockingham Park, April 2, 1985.

406. Mike Recht, "Rockingham Park Feeling Pinch of Casinos, Video Poker Machines," *Union Leader*, May 16, 1995

407. Interview with Edward Callahan. Salem, New Hampshire. June 29, 1996.

408. Damon Runyon, "Lou Smith Cashes In on Personality to Score New Hampshire Racing Beat," *New York Press*. The article is not dated but is likely to originate from the mid to late 1930s. From the scrapbook of Louise Newman.

Index

About the Author

In 1986, Paul Peter Jesep graduated magna cum laude from Union College in Schenectady, New York, with a degree in political science. He earned a law degree three years later from Western New England College School of Law in Springfield, Massachusetts. Mr. Jesep has been admitted to the Connecticut, Massachusetts, Pennsylvania, and New York bars. In 1991, he earned a master of professional studies in political management from the Graduate School of Political Management (GSPM), then in New York City and now based at George Washington University in Washington D.C.

Mr. Jesep is a freelance writer, author of two children's books on Granite State folklore, and a political commentator on local and national issues. He is a resident with his Seal Point Siamese cats, Tristan and Isolde, of Portsmouth, New Hampshire, and makes regular contributions to a variety of publications including, the *Portsmouth Herald*, *HealthCare Review* (a publication for the health care community distributed throughout the six New England states), and *New Hampshire Editions* (a statewide publication on the politics, government, and economy of the Granite State).

He has served as a political consultant, director of legislation for a think tank, staff counsel to a Massachusetts state senator, and political science lecturer at Albertus Magnus College in New Haven, Connecticut and Boston University's Metropolitan College. Currently, he is director of public affairs and government relations for a health care organization serving northern New England.

He is president of the John Paul Jones House Museum/Portsmouth Historical Society. In the past, Mr. Jesep was a member of the New Hampshire Republican State Executive Committee and served as Chair of the Portsmouth, New Hampshire Republican City Committee.

He now serves on the National Executive Committee, National Governing Board, and as president of the New England Chapter of the Ripon Society, a Washington D.C. based think tank of moderate and progressive Republicans.